Daily *warm-ups*

CRITICAL THINKING

J. WESTON
WALCH
PUBLISHER
Portland, Maine

1   2   3   4   5   6   7   8   9   10
ISBN 0-8251-4482-5
Copyright © 2003
J. Weston Walch, Publisher
P.O. Box 658 • Portland, Maine 04104-0658
www.walch.com
Printed in the United States of America

The *Daily Warm-Ups* series is a wonderful way to turn extra classroom minutes into valuable learning time. The 180 quick activities—one for each day of the school year—practice critical-thinking skills in English, Math, Social Studies, Science, and Life Skills. These daily activities may be used at the very beginning of class to get students into learning mode, near the end of class to make good educational use of that transitional time, in the middle of class to shift gears between lessons—or whenever else you have minutes that now go unused. In addition to providing students with structure and focus, they are a natural path to other classroom activities involving critical-thinking skills. As students build their critical-thinking skills, they will be better prepared for standardized tests, such as the PSAT and SAT.

Daily Warm-Ups are easy-to-use reproducibles— simply photocopy the day's activity and distribute it. Or make a transparency of the activity and project it on the board. You may want to use the activities for extra credit points or as a check on the critical-thinking skills that are built and acquired over time.

However you choose to use them, *Daily Warm-Ups* are a convenient and useful supplement to your regular lesson plans. Make every minute of your class time count!

A Spelling Rule Worth Learning

English spelling is often irregular. However, there is one spelling rule that covers a great many words and is almost 100 percent reliable. The rule has to do with whether a word's stressed vowel is long or short. So, if you know how to pronounce a word, the rule will help you spell it correctly. All of the words in the list below follow the rule.

ban	boggle	hidden	pinning	tip
bane	bogus	hide	tap	tipping
bet	den	pin	tape	
better	dentist	pine	tapping	
bog	hid	pining		

What is the rule? Can you think of other words not on the list that follow the rule? Can you think of any English words that do not follow the rule?

1

© 2003 J. Weston Walch, Publisher

Spelling Plurals and Third Persons

Most English nouns add an *s* when they change from singular to plural. So do most verbs when they change from the simple form to the third person. But sometimes the suffix added is pronounced *ez* or *iz* and spelled *es*. Words that end in *y* sometimes <u>change the *y* to *ie* and sometimes don't.</u>

Read the words below. What are rules that govern these changes?

bus, buses	day, days	key, keys	roll, rolls
catch, catches	fish, fishes	kiss, kisses	sprout, sprouts
chick, chicks	fry, fries	laugh, laughs	wish, wishes
	hub, hubs	piano, pianos	
	judge, judges	prize, prizes	

2

Daily Warm-Ups: Critical Thinking

English

How to Succeed in Spelling

All of the words below end with a *seed* sound. Write the rules that
will explain their different spellings.

birdseed	proceed
cottonseed	pumpkinseed
exceed	recede
intercede	secede
linseed	seed
poppyseed	succeed
precede	supersede

3

I Before or After E

I before E
Except after C
Or when pronounced ay
As in "neighbor" and "weigh"

The rhyme above is helpful in spelling many words containing "ie" or "ei," but unfortunately, it does not cover all of them. The following words are spelled correctly.

conceited	foreign	receive	sleight
conceive	forfeit	science	sufficient
efficient	height	shield	weigh
field	protein	sleigh	yield

4

Sort the words into groups as follows: words that follow each of the three parts of the rhymed rule above and words that are exceptions to it. See if you can find one or more extensions to the rule that cover at least some of the exceptions.

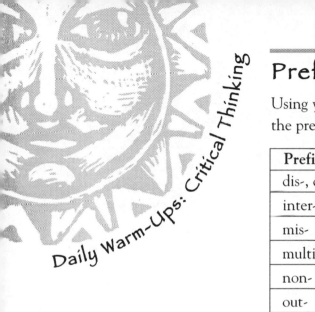

Prefixes

Using your dictionary, find at least three words that have each of the prefixes below.

Prefix	Meaning	Examples
dis-, diff-	away, not	dismiss
inter-	between	interstate
mis-	bad, wrong	misinterpret
multi-	many	multimedia
non-	not	nontoxic
out-	surpass	outvote
over-	beyond the limit	overdraw

Suffixes 1

Using your dictionary, find at least three words that fit into each of the suffix groups below.

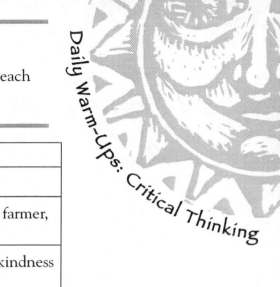

Suffix	Meaning	Examples
-an, -ian	of, from	Canadian
-ary, -er, -ist	one who, that which	missionary, farmer, biologist
-hood, -ness	state, quality of, condition	manhood, kindness
-logy, -ology	discourse, study	psychology
-ment	act, state	movement

6

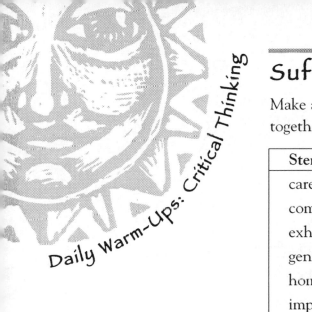

Suffixes 11

Make as many words as you can by putting one of the stems together with one of the suffixes.

Stems	Suffixes
care-	-ful
commerc-	-ive
exhaust-	-ial
gentle-	-ion
home-	-ness
impress-	-ward
polite-	-less
thought-	

7

© 2003 J. Weston Walch, Publisher

Prefixes and Suffixes

Set up a table with a row for each of the prefixes below and a column for each of the suffixes. Using your dictionary, fill in each cell with a word that has the prefix for that row and the suffix for that column.

Prefix	Meaning	Examples
co-, con-	with, together	compress, converge
de-	from, down, away	detach, deodorize
e-, ex-	out of, away, from	external, extraordinary
i-, in-	in, into	input, illuminate
pro-	for, forward	project, progress, pronuclear
re-	back, again	return, reverse

Suffix	Meaning	Examples
-ary, -ory	of, like, relating to, being	missionary, observatory
-ative, -ent, -ive,	of, like, relating to, being	conservative, decadent, active
-able, -ible	capable of, worthy of	payable, visible

8

Scrambled Words I

There is a sentence that uses all of the words below and no others and exactly two punctuation marks: a comma and a period.

and	Livvie	post	the
besides	market	Saari's	to
Cove	office	store	village
down	only	the	walked
in	past	the	was
Lane's	past	the	which

Reconstruct the sentence.

9

Scrambled Words 11

There is a sentence that uses all of the words below and no others
and exactly one punctuation mark: a period.

A	enclosed	lobstermen	silver
a	fishermen	made	small
and	for	of	the
blocks	granite	of	the
breakwater	harbor	of	
craft	huge	quiet	

Reconstruct the sentence.

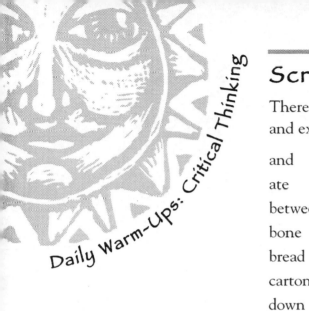

Scrambled Words III

There is a sentence that uses all of the words below and no others and exactly four punctuation marks: three commas and a period.

and	fish	milk	the
ate	fish	of	the
between	fried	put	the
bone	from	quickly	washing
bread	He	removed	with
carton	it	slices	
down	it	the	

Reconstruct the sentence.

11

Scrambled Words IV

There are two sentences that use all of the words below and no others and exactly three punctuation marks: one comma and two periods.

and	Finally	She	the	tried
at	go	she	to	twinkling
back	got	sleep	to	up
but	kindly	stars	to	went
couldn't	look	the	to	window

Reconstruct the sentences.

12

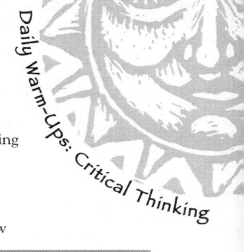

The Good, the Bad, and the Sloppy

No two words mean exactly the same thing, but words that have similar meanings are called synonyms.

Sort the words in the list below into groups of synonyms.

acceptable	enduring	good	offensive
agreeable	excellent	intolerable	powerful
beneficial	favorable	lousy	revolting
cautious	finicky	mischievous	robust
desirable	forceful	muscular	
detrimental	fussy	obnoxious	

Daily Warm-Ups: Critical Thinking

13

Work, Play, and Travel

No two words mean exactly the same thing, but words that have similar meanings are called synonyms.

Sort the words in the list below into groups of synonyms.

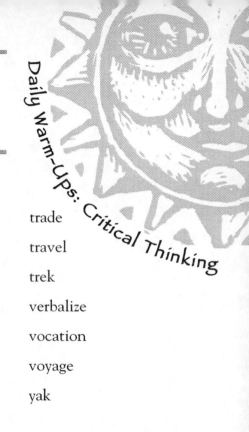

Daily Warm-Ups: Critical Thinking

amusement	business	employment	occupation	trade
art	calling	enjoyment	pleasure	travel
assignment	car	entertainment	proceed	trek
	chat	explore	profession	verbalize
	chore	fun	recreation	vocation
	converse	gab	roam	voyage
	craft	job	speak	yak
	cruise	journey	sport	
	delight	labor	talk	
	duty	move	toil	

14

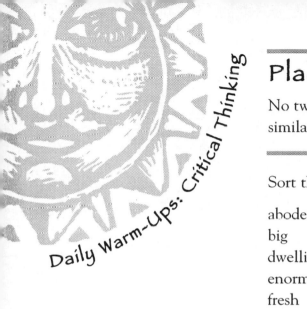

English

Places, Great and Small

No two words mean exactly the same thing, but words that have similar meanings are called synonyms.

Sort the words in the list below into groups of synonyms.

abode	huge	novel	trivial
big	hulking	petite	vast
dwelling	immense	piddling	voluminous
enormous	large	puny	whopping
fresh	little	recent	
great	major	residence	
heap	mound	sizable	
hill	mountain	small	
home	new	tiny	

15

Animal Rage

No two words mean exactly the same thing, but words that have similar meanings are called synonyms.

Sort the words in the list below into groups of synonyms.

animal	bother	irritation	soul
annoy	creature	mad	stress
annoyance	distress	mortal	temper
beast	fauna	pain	trouble
	harass	person	vex
	human	pique	wrath
	individual	rage	
	irk	someone	

16

Scrambled Sentences 1

Daily Warm-Ups: Critical Thinking

In the news story below, the order of the sentences has been scrambled.

1. The board named Gunter Thielen, a long-time executive and head of the Bertelsmann Foundation, its new chief executive.

2. The company said there were "differences of opinion" between Mr. Middelhoff and the board "over the future strategy of Bertelsmann."

3. In the latest eruption of boardroom turmoil at a global media conglomerate, the chairman and chief executive of Bertelsmann of Germany, Thomas Middelhoff, was unexpectedly ousted today.

4. Bertelsmann dismissed Mr. Middelhoff this evening at a meeting of its board.

17

In the original story, the sentence that delivers the point of the story came first. The sentences that support the point with details came after it. What do you think the order of sentences was in the original story? Why?

Scrambled Sentences II

In the news story below, the order of the sentences has been scrambled.

1. Work on a permanent system for regulating traffic was interrupted by the September 11 attacks.

2. The departing administrator of the Federal Aviation Administration is urging Congress to let the agency ration flights at busy airports like La Guardia.

3. But another reason for the delay in a permanent system is doubt that the agency has the authority to decide who may use an airport when airline demand exceeds the airport's capacity.

4. Jane F. Garvey, whose five-year term as administrator ends on August 4, recently extended for two years a stopgap lottery system that was begun at La Guardia in 2001 to limit congestion and delays.

18

In the original story, the sentence that delivers the point of the story came first. The sentences that support the point with details came after it. What do you think the order of sentences was in the original story? Why?

Scrambled Sentences III

In the news story below, the order of the sentences has been scrambled.

1. "Three days might have been valuable in the past but times have changed," Deputy State Registrar Lorraine Wilson said.

2. The new law that went into effect last week eliminates the three-day waiting period after obtaining a marriage license.

3. Couples can fill out the paperwork and get married the same day in Maine thanks to changes in state law, the first overhaul of the state's marriage laws since the 1950s.

4. In addition to eliminating delays, Maine's new statute removes the requirement that a bride and groom who live in different towns file paperwork in both places.

19

In the original story, the sentence that delivers the point of the story came first. The sentences that support the point with details came after it. What do you think the order of sentences was in the original story? Why?

Scrambled Sentences IV

In the news story below, the order of the sentences has been scrambled.

1. It is an inning where the defense seems to fall apart, and the pitcher can't seem to get the ball over the plate.

2. To win, you need to find a way to cut down on those nerve-racking innings.

3. Big innings are common throughout baseball, not just Little League.

4. There is an axiom in youth baseball that every team seems to experience one bad inning on defense in most games.

5. Just being aware of that one bad inning will sometimes help.

20

In the original story, the sentence that delivers the point of the story came first. The sentences that support the point with details came after it. What do you think the order of sentences was in the original story? Why?

Daily Warm-Ups: Critical Thinking

The Mountain Can Fly

Words are grammatically substitutable if they can appear in the same place in the same sentence without making the sentence grammatically wrong. For example, in the list below, *bird* and *mountain* are grammatically substitutable because "The bird can fly" and "The mountain can fly" are both grammatical sentences (though mountains can't really fly). *Bird* and *very* are not grammatically substitutable because "The very can fly" is not a grammatical sentence.

a	fly	procrastinate	see	will
beautiful	handle	really	ship	
bird	large	red	the	
can	lovely	remain	too	
could	mountain	run	toothbrush	
faint	my	Sam's	very	

21

Sort the words in the list above into sets of words that are grammatically substitutable for each other. (Some words will go into more than one set.) Then write some funny, but grammatically correct, sentences using substitutable words. Try to write your sentences so that you create as few substitution sets as possible.

This Tree Would Evaporate Slowly

Two words are grammatically substitutable if they can both appear in the same place in the same sentence without making the sentence grammatically wrong. For example, in the list below, *water* and *tree* are grammatically substitutable because "This water would evaporate slowly" and "This tree would evaporate slowly" are both grammatical sentences. (Don't worry about the fact that trees can't really evaporate.) On the other hand, *water* and *under* are not grammatically substitutable because "This under would evaporate slowly" is not a grammatical sentence.

a	friend	light	over	tree
arrive	gracefully	may	sink	water
bicycle	green	must	sleep	would
evaporate	heavy	old	slowly	
fall	his	on	this	

22

Sort the words in the list above into sets of words that are grammatically substitutable for each other. Then write some funny, but grammatically correct, sentences using substitutable words. Try to write your sentences so that you create as few substitution sets as possible.

Tigers Frown

Two words are grammatically substitutable if they can both appear in the same place in the same sentence without making the sentence grammatically wrong. For example, in the list below, *tigers* and *sockets* are grammatically substitutable because "Tigers frown" and "Sockets frown" are both grammatical sentences. (Don't worry about the fact that sockets can't really frown.) On the other hand, *tiger* and *throw* are not grammatically substitutable because "Throw frown" is not a grammatical sentence.

backpacks	float	intelligent	walk
collapse	frown	sockets	yellow
dump	funny	steal	
empty	hit	throw	
faucets	huge	tigers	

23

Sort the words in the list above into sets of words that are grammatically substitutable for each other. Then write some funny, but grammatically correct, sentences using substitutable words. Try to write your sentences so that you create as few substitution sets as possible.

My Dress Crushed Myron's Dumpster

Words are grammatically substitutable if they can appear in the same place in the same sentence without making the sentence grammatically wrong. For example, in the list below, *cannon* and *dress* are grammatically substitutable because "My cannon crushed Myron's dumpster" and "My dress crushed Myron's dumpster" are both grammatical sentences (though a dress can't really crush a dumpster). On the other hand, *cannon* and *and* are not grammatically substitutable because "My and crushed Myron's dumpster" is not a grammatical sentence.

24

admired	cheap	incredible	wide
and	crushed	my	window
black	dress	Myron's	your
but	dumpster	or	
cannon	empty	painted	

Sort the words in the list above into sets of words that are grammatically substitutable for each other. Then write some funny, but grammatically correct, sentences using substitutable words. Try to write your sentences so that you create as few substitution sets as possible.

Daily Warm-Ups: Critical Thinking

It Is Not Growing Like a Tree

It is not growing like a tree
In bulk, doth make man better be;
Or standing long an oak, three hundred year,
To fall a log at last, dry, bald, and sere:
A lily of a day
Is fairer far in May
Although it fall and die that night;
It was the plant and flower of light.
In small proportions we just beauties see;
And in short measures, life may perfect be.

—Ben Jonson (1573–1637)

25

Paraphrase the poem above. To paraphrase a text means to express its meaning in your own words.

Success

Success is counted sweetest
By those who ne'er succeed.
To comprehend a nectar
Requires sorest need.

Not one of all the purple Host
Who took the Flag today
Can tell the definition
So clear of Victory

As he defeated—dying—
On whose forbidden ear
The distant strains of triumph
Burst agonized and clear!

—Emily Dickinson (1830–1886)

26

Paraphrase the poem above. To paraphrase a text means to express its meaning in your own words.

Upon Jone and Jane

Jone is a wench that's painted;
Jone is a girl that's tainted;
Yet Jone she goes
Like one of those
Whom purity had Sainted.

Jane is a girl that's prittie;
Jane is a wench that's wittie;
Yet, who wo'd think,
Her breath do's stinke,
As so it doth? that's pittie.

—Robert Herrick (1591–1674)

Paraphrase the poem above. To paraphrase a text means to express its meaning in your own words.

27

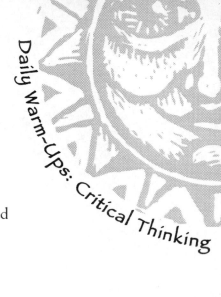

When I Heard the Learn'd Astronomer

When I heard the learn'd astronomer,
When the proofs, the figures, were ranged in columns before me,
When I was shown the charts and diagrams, to add, divide, and measure them,
When I sitting heard the astronomer where he lectured with much applause in the lecture-room,
How soon, unaccountable, I became tired and sick,
Till rising and gliding out I wander'd off by myself,
In the mystical moist night-air, and from time to time,
Look'd up in perfect silence at the stars.

—Walt Whitman (1819–1992)

Paraphrase the poem above. To paraphrase a text means to express its meaning in your own words.

Daily Warm-Ups: Critical Thinking

Arriving at Moral Perfection

"I conceiv'd the bold and arduous project of arriving at moral perfection. I wish'd to live without committing any fault at any time; I would conquer all that either natural inclination, custom, or company might lead me into. As I knew, or thought I knew, what was right and wrong, I did not see why I might not always do the one and avoid the other. But I soon found I had undertaken a task of more difficulty than I had imagined. While my care was employ'd in guarding against one fault, I was often surprised by another; habit took the advantage of inattention; inclination was sometimes too strong for reason. I concluded, at length, that the mere speculative conviction that it was our interest to be completely virtuous, was not sufficient to prevent our slipping…"

—from *The Autobiography* by Benjamin Franklin (1706–1790)

Recall and write about a time in your life when you had the same kind of difficulty Franklin had.

29

American Cookery

"There is a familiar and too much despised branch of civilization, of which the population of this country is singularly and unhappily ignorant; that of cookery. The Americans are the grossest feeders of any civilized nation known. As a nation, their food is heavy, coarse, ill-prepared and indigestible, while it is taken in the least artificial forms that cookery will allow. The predominance of grease in the American kitchen, coupled with the habits of hasty eating and of constant expectoration, are the causes of the diseases of the stomach so common in America."

—from *The American Democrat* by James Fenimore Cooper (1789–1851)

30

Cooper published *The American Democrat* in 1838. Suppose he were writing today. Would the above be fair and accurate? Why or why not?

Self-Reliance

"There is a time in every man's education when he arrives at the conviction that envy is ignorance; that imitation is suicide; that he must take himself for better for worse as his portion; that though the wide universe is full of good, no kernel of nourishing corn can come to him but through his toil on that plot of ground which is given to him to till. The power which resides in him is new in nature, and none but he knows what that is which he can do, nor does he know until he has tried."

—from "Self-Reliance" by Ralph Waldo Emerson (1803–1882)

Emerson wrote "Self-Reliance" in 1841. Does what he says above have any validity today? Why or why not?

31

Reading List

Literature is an important part of English class. How do you think teachers should decide what books to teach? If you were teaching your grade, what books would you include on a summer reading list, and why? Write your answers below.

English

How to Be Popular

"There are two opposite ways by which some men get into notice—one by talking a vast deal and thinking a little, and the other by holding their tongues and not thinking at all. By the first many a vapouring superficial pretender acquires the reputation of a man of quick parts—by the other many a vacant dunderpate, like the owl, the stupidest of birds, comes to be complimented, by a discerning world, with all the attributes of wisdom."

—Washington Irving (1783–1859)

Do you agree with this writer's understanding of how people get to be popular? Why or why not?

George Washington and the Cherry Tree

"George," said his father, "do you know who killed that beautiful little cherry tree yonder in the garden?" This was a tough question, and George staggered under it for a moment but quickly recovered himself. Looking at his father, with the sweet face of youth brightened with the inexpressible charm of all-conquering truth, he bravely cried out, "I can't tell a lie, Pa. You know I can't tell a lie. I did cut it with my hatchet." "Run to my arms, you dearest boy," cried his father in transports, "run to my arms! Glad am I, George, that you killed my tree for you have paid me for it a thousand fold. Such an act of heroism in my son is worth more than a thousand trees, though blossomed with silver and their fruits of purest gold."

—Mason Locke Weems (1759-1825)

Do you believe this story? Why or why not? If you do believe it, how do you explain it? If you don't believe it, why do you think someone would make it up?

Daily Warm-Ups: Critical Thinking

Cabbages and Kings

"They will tell you in Anchuria, that President Miraflores, of that volatile republic, died by his own hand in the coast town of Coralio; that he had reached thus far in flight from the inconveniences of an imminent revolution; and that one hundred thousand dollars, government funds, which he carried with him in an American leather valise as a souvenir of his tempestuous administration, was never afterward recovered."

Fiction writers often give you a general idea in the first few paragraphs of a short story or novel of what the story to follow will be about. The paragraph above is the beginning of a novel called *Cabbages and Kings* by O. Henry (1862–1910). What do you think happens in the story?

35

Compensation

"For everything you have missed, you have gained something else;
and for everything you gain, you lose something else."

—Ralph Waldo Emerson (1803–1882)

Daily Warm-Ups: Critical Thinking

Do you agree? Do you think there is some sort of balance for human
beings, as there seems to be in nature? Explain, using examples from
your own experience and/or from historical events.

36

Big Numbers, Small Numbers 1

Arrange the numbers below in order from smallest to largest. Use a calculator if you wish.

3.5×10^9	6.28×10^7
1,000,000	8,765,243,778,625
128	9.9838×10^7
$9\frac{3}{4}$	0.3333
4.08×10^{-4}	0.000832
0	$\frac{1}{7}$
76,922	$\frac{1}{3000}$

37

Big Numbers, Small Numbers 11

Arrange the numbers below in order from smallest to largest. Use a calculator if you wish.

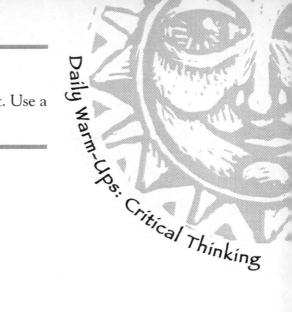

$\dfrac{91}{635}$	$\dfrac{96}{209}$	$\dfrac{21}{62}$
$\dfrac{13}{41}$	$\dfrac{450}{463}$	$\dfrac{24}{407}$
0	$\dfrac{91}{635}$	$\dfrac{67}{302}$
1	$\dfrac{627}{797}$	
$\dfrac{59}{180}$		

38

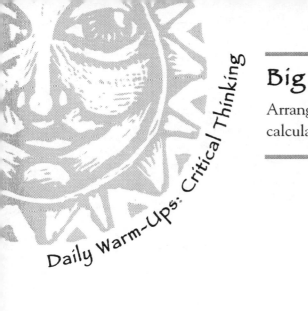

Big Numbers, Small Numbers III

Arrange the numbers below in order from smallest to largest. Use a calculator if you wish.

−70.060	46.372
−26.314	66.275
−35.127	70.757
87.548	27.891
−18.294	−9.686

39

Og's Shopping Trip

Og travels to Alexandrov, a nearby planet, to shop.

Og has to buy five crash neutralizers, which cost 900 D each, a navigational software update, 5 KD, 17 new energy modules at 30 D each, and 432 D worth of replacement parts for his spaceship. D is the abbreviation for drov, the smallest unit of money; KD is for kilodrov or 1,000 drovs.

In order to buy this merchandise, Og must exchange the money he brought with him, which is in shekels, the currency of his home planet, to drovs. The exchange rate is 1.45 shekels per drov.

Write a mathematical sentence that expresses the amount of money in shekels Og will have to exchange to buy what he needs.

Teen Drinking on the Increase

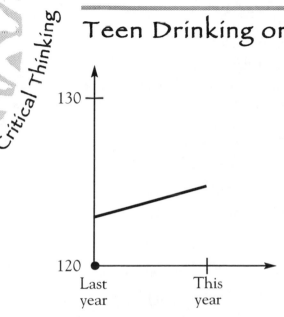

This graph shows how many students at Central High School admitted on surveys this year and last year that they had drunk an alcoholic beverage in the preceding month. As you can see, there has been a sharp increase. Parents and school officials must immediately put in place a program to fight this growing menace to our children's health and safety.

There were 2,400 students enrolled at Central High last year and 2,415 this year.

Daily Warm-Ups: Critical Thinking

41

Do you agree with the above interpretation of the survey data? Explain why or why not.

2 = 1

Most people are not aware that 2 = 1. However, here is the proof. Suppose *a* and *b* are any two numbers as long as they are equal to each other.

$a = b$. If we multiply each side by a, we get

$a^2 = ab$. Adding a^2 to each side, we get

$a^2 + a^2 = a^2 + ab$. We can rewrite that as

$2a^2 = a^2 + ab$. Now if we subtract $2ab$ from each side we get

$2a^2 - 2ab = a^2 + ab - 2ab$. Adding like terms, we get

$2a^2 - 2ab = a^2 - ab$. Factoring, we can rewrite this as

$2(a^2 - ab) = 1(a^2 - ab)$. Now if we divide each side by $a^2 - ab$, we get

$2 = 1$.

42

Now that you have seen the proof, do you believe that 2 = 1? If not, why not?

The Next Flip of the Coin

You flip a coin. It comes up heads ten times in a row.

What is the probability that when you flip it the next time it will come up heads? Explain why.

43

Rolling the Dice

When you roll standard dice, what are the chances that the sum of the two dice will be an even number? What are the chances that the product of the two dice will be an even number? Explain your answer.

44

One Letter After Another

The letters A, B, C, D, and E can be combined in three-letter groups—for example, ABC, EDB, ACE, and so on—in 60 possible ways.

Is the above statement true? What assumption do you have to make for it to be true?

Daily Warm-Ups: Critical Thinking

45

Making Rectangles 1

Draw and label a rectangle that has the same area as the one below and a greater perimeter. Prove that it does.

3 cm

4 cm

46

Making Rectangles 11

Draw and label a rectangle that has the same area as the triangle below and a greater perimeter. Prove that it does.

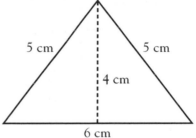

5 cm   5 cm

4 cm

6 cm

47

Making Rectangles III

Draw and label a rectangle that has less area than the circle below and a perimeter greater than its circumference. Prove that it does.

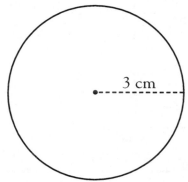

3 cm

48

Math

Size and Weight Classification 1

Think of objects that fall into these four classes:

1. 1 foot or larger in at least one dimension,

2. Smaller than 1 foot in all dimensions,

3. Weighing 8 pounds or more,

4. Lighter than 8 pounds.

There should be at least three objects in each class.

Draw a Venn diagram with two overlapping circles representing classes 2 and 4. Write the objects in the appropriate places in the Venn diagram.

49

Math

Size and Weight Classification II

Think of objects that fall into these four classes:

1. 1 centimeter or larger in at least one dimension,

2. Smaller than 1 centimeter in all dimensions,

3. Weighing 1 gram or more,

4. Lighter than 1 gram.

There should be at least three objects in each class.

Draw a Venn diagram with two overlapping circles representing classes 2 and 4. Write the objects in the appropriate places in the Venn diagram.

50

Toothpick Geometry

Write a set of directions to tell a classmate how to make the geometric figure below using eight toothpicks. The classmate is not allowed to see the figure.

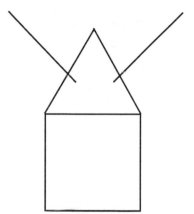

51

Polygon Words

Think of 15 words that are related to polygons in some way. Then sort the words into groups that are similar. Label each group.

Daily Warm-Ups: Critical Thinking

52

Daily Warm-Ups: Critical Thinking

Measurement Word Sort

All of the words below have to do with some kind of measurement.

centimeter	kilometer	ounce
degree	light year	stopwatch
gallon	measuring cup	thermometer
gram	measuring tape	ton
hour	mile	
inch	minute	

Sort the words according to how or what they measure. Label each group.

53

Number Riddles

Here's a number riddle. I'm thinking of a two-digit odd number. The sum of its digits is 13. It is a multiple of 7. What is the number?

Answer the riddle and then make up one of your own.

54

Math

What Could Happen?

Think about the next year of your life. Can you think of three events for each of these categories?

1. Certain to happen

2. Likely but not certain

3. Unlikely but not impossible

4. Impossible

55

© 2003 J. Weston Walch, Publisher

Real-World Solid Figures

List up to five objects found in the real world that have the shapes of each of the following solid figures:

- Prism

- Cube

- Pyramid

- Cylinder

- Cone

- Sphere

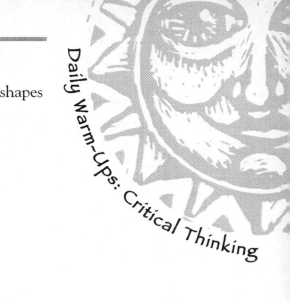

56

Daily Warm-Ups: Critical Thinking

Write Your Own Word Problem 1

Here's a word problem that can be solved using multiplication: Larnel has $1.50. The game he wants to buy costs 5 times as much. How much more does Larnel have to save to buy the game?

Here's one way to solve it. Let g = the cost of the game Larnel wants to buy. It costs 5 times as much as Larnel has. Larnel has $1.50. So $g = 5(\$1.50)$. Larnel has to save up $g - \$1.50 = 5(\$1.50) - \$1.50 = \$7.50 - \$1.50 = \$6.00$.

Write a word problem that can be solved using multiplication.

57

Write Your Own Word Problem II

Here's a word problem that can be solved using division: Maya and her two friends made cookies and sold them at a festival. They took in $21. Each person did about the same amount of work on the project. Maya spent $3 on the ingredients. So they agreed to reimburse Maya and then split what's left equally. How much does each person get?

Here's a way to solve it. Let s = each person's share of the profits.

$$s = \frac{(\$21 - \$3)}{3} = \frac{\$18}{3} = \$6$$

Write a word problem that can be solved using division.

58

Daily Warm-Ups: Critical Thinking

Write Your Own Word Problem III

Here's a word problem that can be solved using two equations. Three large chunks of cheese and two small chunks of cheese weigh 4.2 kg. Four large chunks and three small chunks weigh 5.8 kg. How much do two large chunks and one small chunk weigh?

Here's a solution:
Let b = the weight of a large chunk and s = the weight of a small chunk.

$3b + 2s = 4.2$ kg ⟶ Multiplying both sides by 3 ⟶ $9b + 6s = 12.6$ kg

$4b + 3s = 5.8$ kg ⟶ Multiplying both sides by 2 ⟶ $8b + 6s = 11.6$ kg

Subtracting $\qquad\qquad\qquad\qquad\quad b = 1$kg

Substituting in the first equation 3 kg $+ 2s = 4.2$ kg

Subtracting 3 kg from both sides $\qquad\quad 2s = 1.2$ kg

Dividing both sides by 2 $\qquad\qquad\qquad s = 0.6$ kg

Two large chunks weigh 2 kg. One small chunk weighs 0.6 kg. Two large chunks and one small chunk weigh 2.6 kg.

59

Write your own word problem that can be solved using two equations.

What Is Place Value?

Write a paragraph explaining what place value is and how it works.
Give examples.

60

Math

What Is a Tessellation?

Write a paragraph explaining what a tessellation is.
Draw an example.

Daily Warm-Ups: Critical Thinking

61

What Is a Rational Number?

Write a paragraph explaining what a rational number is.
Give examples.

62

Math

How to Multiply Fractions

Explain how to multiply fractions. Give an example.

63

Math

How to Divide Fractions

Explain how to divide one fraction by another. Give an example.

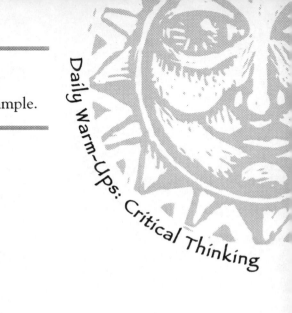

Daily Warm-Ups: Critical Thinking

64

© 2003 J. Weston Walch, Publisher

How to Add Fractions with Like Denominators

Explain how to add fractions with like denominators. Give an example.

65

How to Add Fractions with Unlike Denominators

Explain how to add fractions with unlike denominators. Give an example.

66

Daily Warm-Ups: Critical Thinking

Here's the Headline, You Write the Story 1

The headline of a news story summarizes it in a few words. If you want to find out the details, you have to read the story. The equation for a word problem is like the headline of a news story. Here's an example.

Equation: $5x + 10 = 35$

Word problem: Marcia's employer paid her $35, her pay for working 5 hours plus $10 for some things that she bought for him at the store. How much did Marcia get paid per hour?

Here's the headline: $15 \times 20 - 14 \times 19 = x$. You write the story.

67

Here's the Headline, You Write the Story II

The headline of a news story summarizes it in a few words. If you want to find out the details, you have to read the story. The equation for a word problem is like the headline of a news story. Here's an example.

Equation: $5x + 10 = 35$

Word problem: Marcia's employer paid her $35, her pay for working 5 hours plus $10 for some things that she bought for him at the store. How much did Marcia get paid per hour?

68

Here's the headline: $x - 4 \times 9.95 - 1.99 = \$8.21$. You write the story.

Here's the Headline, You Write the Story III

The headline of a news story summarizes it in a few words. If you want to find out the details, you have to read the story. The equation for a word problem is like the headline of a news story. Here's an example.

Equation: $5x + 10 = 35$

Word problem: Marcia's employer gave her $35, her pay for working 5 hours plus $10 for some things that she bought for him at the store. How much did Marcia get paid per hour?

Here's the headline: $\frac{x}{2} - 8 = 10$. You write the story.

69

How Many Colors Does It Take to Make a Map?

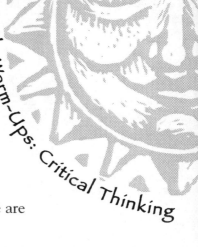

Daily Warm-Ups: Critical Thinking

Maps of the world use different colors so that you can see clearly where one country ends and another begins. It has been said that if you follow certain rules for drawing the boundaries of countries, every map you draw can be colored with only two colors. These are the rules: Start drawing at any point on a sheet of paper. You may move your pencil to any point on the paper, but you may not stop or lift your pencil off the paper until you return to the point where you started. Here are two examples:

70

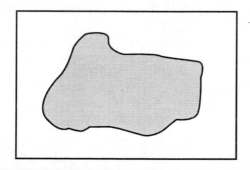

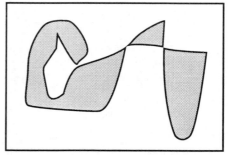

Do the rules work? Experiment and explain why or why not.

How Many Colors Does It Take to Make a Map? II

A second map coloring experiment uses the following rules. Every time you draw a boundary, you may start at any point. You may move your pencil to any point on the paper, but you may not stop or lift your pencil off the paper until you return to the point where you started. But you may draw as many loops as you want. And they can overlap as much as you want. Here are two examples:

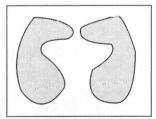
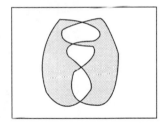

It has been said that if you follow the boundary drawing rules above, every map you draw can be colored with only two colors. Do you believe that? Experiment and explain why or why not.

71

How Many Colors Does It Take to Make a Map? III

A third map coloring experiment uses these rules. Every time you draw a boundary, you may start at any point. You do not need to return to the point where you started. But if a country shares a border with another country, it must be a different color. Here is an example that only uses four colors.

72

If you follow the rule above, how many colors does it take to draw a map? Can every possible map be drawn with only four colors? Or are there some possible maps that need five or more? What do you think? If you have coloring tools, use them to experiment. If not, simulate colors using shading as in the example above.

Fiction and History

There are many genres (types) of fiction, including historical fiction, fantasy, mysteries, science fiction, romance, poetry, and adventure stories. There are a variety of nonfiction writings, too: biographies, autobiographies, diaries, essays, letters, news reports, textbooks, and so on.

Do you think it is useful for a social studies class to read fiction as well as nonfiction? What might you get from reading fiction as well as nonfiction?

73

Daily Warm-Ups: Critical Thinking

My Era

Imagine that students years from now are reading a social studies text about the early twenty-first century. What three events do you think will be highlighted in the text? Why?

Daily Warm-Ups: Critical Thinking

74

Daily Warm-Ups: Critical Thinking

Social Studies

Gandhi's Theory

Read Mohandas Gandhi's explanation of nonviolence.

"Non-violence does not mean making peace. On the other hand, it means fighting bravely and sincerely for truth and doing what is just. The doctrine of Satyagraha (civil disobedience) works on the principle that you make the so-called enemy see and realize the injustice he is engaged in. It can work only when you believe in God and the goodness of the people to see that they are wrong. As a satyagrahi, I do believe that non-violence is a potent weapon against all evils. I warn you, however, that the victory will not come easy—just like it will not come easy with violent methods such as fighting with weaponry."

What do you think of nonviolence and civil disobedience? Do you see any situations in today's world where it might be applicable?

75

Family Law Among the Mesopotamians

This is an excerpt from laws of ancient Mesopotamia (c. 2250–550 B.C.E.):

"Be it enacted forever and for all future days: If a son says to his father, 'You are not my father,' he [the father] can cut off his [the son's] locks, make him a slave and sell him for money… If a father says to his son, 'You are not my son,' the latter has to leave house and field and he loses everything. If a wife is unfaithful to her husband and then says, 'You are not my husband,' let her be thrown into the river. If a husband says to his wife, 'You are not my wife,' he shall as a fine pay one half mana of silver."

Daily Warm-Ups: Critical Thinking

From this text and your knowledge of history, what can you tell about family life in ancient Mesopotamia?

76

Going Too Far

"True, the peasants are in a sense 'unruly' in the countryside. Supreme in authority, the peasant association allows the landlord no say and sweeps away his prestige. People swarm into the houses of local tyrants and evil gentry who are against the peasant association, slaughter their pigs and consume their grain. They even loll for a minute or two on the ivory-inlaid beds belonging to the young ladies in the households of the local tyrants and evil gentry. At the slightest provocation they make arrests, crown the arrested with tall paper hats, and parade them through the villages, saying, 'You dirty landlords, now you know who we are!' Doing whatever they like and turning everything upside down, they have created a kind of terror in the countryside. This is what some people call 'going too far.'"

77

From the text and your knowledge of history, what can you tell about the situation being described? What is the author's point of view on it?

How Many Americans Are Poor?

The U.S. Census measures the number and percentage of people who are poor in terms of household income thresholds that take into account the number of people in a household and their ages. For example, if a family of four with two children under 18 has a total annual income of $17,524 or less, then the family is considered poor and every member of it is counted as poor. This graph shows how poverty levels changed from 1959 to 2000.

Daily Warm-Ups: Critical Thinking

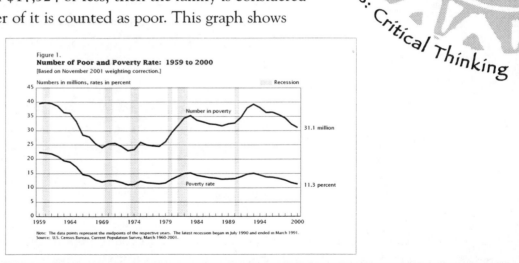

Figure 1.
Number of Poor and Poverty Rate: 1959 to 2000
[Based on November 2001 weighting correction.]

Numbers in millions, rates in percent | Recession

Number in poverty

31.1 million

Poverty rate

11.3 percent

Note: The data points represent the midpoints of the respective years. The latest recession began in July 1990 and ended in March 1991.
Source: U.S. Census Bureau, Current Population Survey, March 1960-2001.

78

Is the information in the graph above good news or bad news? What, if anything, should be done about it?

Social Studies

Planning the Commandant's Trip

The Commandant of the United States Marine Corps, whose headquarters is in Washington, DC, wishes to fly to the U.S. embassies in several countries to inspect Marine guards and then return to Washington. Here are the countries: Australia, Chile, China, Finland, Iceland, Malaysia, Pakistan, Syria, and Trinidad and Tobago. Your job is to plan the commandant's trip so as to conserve fuel and flight time as much as possible. In which order should the commandant visit the embassies?

79

Violent Crime

This graph shows the number of people 12 or older per thousand per year who were victims of violent crimes. The data are from the National Crime Victimization Survey of 80,000 people who have been interviewed twice per year since 1972 and asked if they were victims of rape, robbery, or assault. The data also includes homicide statistics from the FBI Uniform Crime Reports.

Daily Warm-Ups: Critical Thinking

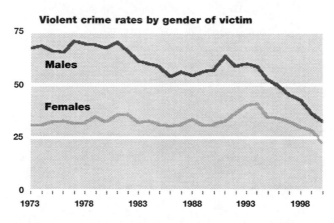

Violent crime rates by gender of victim

80

Write a news story with a headline explaining this graph and its significance.

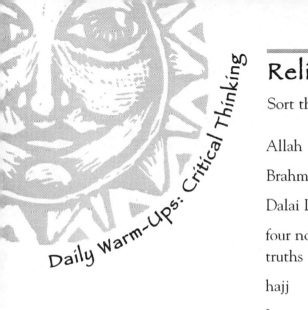

Religion Word Sort 1

Sort the words below according to the religion they relate to.

Allah

Brahma

Dalai Llama

four noble truths

hajj

Jesus

Krishna

Mecca

Muhammad

New Testament

nirvana

Old Testament

Passover

Qur'an

Ramadan

resurrection

right livelihood

sabbath

sacraments

Shiva

Talmud

Torah

Trinity

Veda

Vishnu

Yom Kippur

81

© 2003 J. Weston Walch, Publisher

Daily Warm-Ups: Critical Thinking

Religion Word Sort II

Sort the following places according to the dominant religion(s) practiced in them.

Africa	Indonesia	Malaysia
Albania	Iran	Pakistan
Algeria	Iraq	Sri Lanka
China	Israel	Tibet
Egypt	Japan	Turkey
Europe	Jordan	
India	Korea	

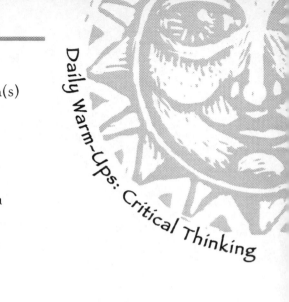

Daily Warm-Ups: Critical Thinking

82

Eastern Mediterranean Word Sort

Sort the words below according to the region or time period they relate to. Label each group.

Abraham	fire	mummy	sea trade
alphabet	Hammurabi	Nile	stone tools
Assyria	hunting	nomadic	Sumer
Babylon	Israel	pharaoh	Tigris
Canaan	Jerusalem	Phoenicia	writing
Egypt	Mesopotamia	prehistory	
Euphrates	Moses	pyramid	

83

Asia Word Sort

Sort the words below into two groups, India and China.

acupuncture   Himalayas

Buddhism   Hindu

Chandragupta   Indus

Confucius   paper

Ganges   Sanskrit

Great Wall   Silk Road

Han Dynasty

Daily Warm-Ups: Critical Thinking

84

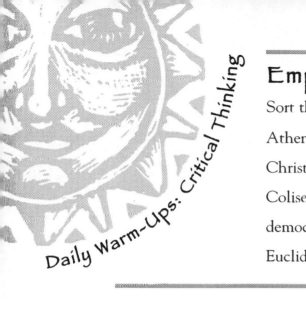

Empire Word Sort

Sort the words below into two groups, Greece and Rome.

Athens

Christianity

Coliseum

democracy

Euclid

Homer

Italy

Julius Caesar

Latin

Olympic Games

philosophy

Socrates

Sparta

Trojan War

85

Daily Warm-Ups: Critical Thinking

Geography Word Sort

Sort the words below according to their meanings. Label each group.

1500 Pleasant St.	mountain
airport	movement
city	ocean
country	place
dam	plain
farming	region
hill	road
human/environment interaction	state
lake	town
latitude	train
location	tundra
mining	valley

86

Time Travel I

Imagine you have the opportunity to travel to a time and place in the past. When you get there, you will be the same age and gender you are now. You will live in a family roughly comparable to the one you live in now. You will not be able to do anything that might affect later events. Otherwise, though, you will participate in the life of the time and place as if you belonged there.

Where and when would you go? Why? What would your life be like?

Time Travel II

Imagine that you are going to travel back in time to when your parents were the age that you are now. Choose one parent whose background fascinates you for the trip. You will live in the family and community your parent lived in. You will not be able to do anything that might affect later events. Otherwise, though, you will participate in the life of the time and place as if you belonged there.

Where and when would you go? What would your life be like there?

Daily Warm-Ups: Critical Thinking

88

Daily Warm-Ups: Critical Thinking

Social Studies

Time Travel III

Imagine that you are going to travel back in time to when your grandparents were the age that you are now. Choose one of your grandparents for the trip. You will live in the family and community your grandparent lived in. You will not be able to do anything that might affect later events. Otherwise, though, you will participate in the life of the time and place as if you belonged there.

Where and when would you go? What would your life be like there?

89

© 2003 J. Weston Walch, Publisher

Time Travel IV

Imagine that you are going to travel to the time in the future when your children will be the age that you are now. When you get there, you will be the same age and gender you are now. You will live in the family and community your children live in. You will participate in the life of the time and place as if you belonged there.

Where will your children be? What year will it be? What will your life be like there?

90

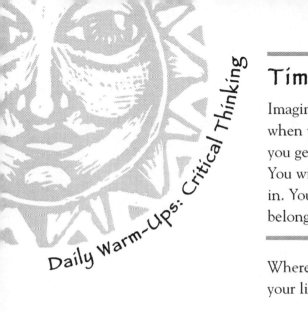

Social Studies

Time Travel V

Imagine that you are going to travel to the time in the future when your grandchildren will be the age that you are now. When you get there, you will be the same age and gender you are now. You will live in the family and community your grandchildren live in. You will participate in the life of the time and place as if you belonged there.

Where will your grandchildren be? What year will it be? What will your life be like there?

91

© 2003 J. Weston Walch, Publisher

Future Technology

Fifty years ago, telephone calls were much more expensive than they are today. Telephones only worked if they were connected by a wire to the telephone network. There was no voice mail. The quality of the sound transmitted was often poor. Automobiles were much slower, less safe, less fuel efficient, and more polluting than they are today.

Think of a technology that we have today and imagine that in the future it improves as much as the telephone and the automobile have in the past fifty years. What will it be like? How will people's lives be different because of the improved technology?

Daily Warm-Ups: Critical Thinking

92

Daily Warm-Ups: Critical Thinking

Social Studies

Globalization

In 2002, two neighboring countries, India and Pakistan, came close to going to war. One reason they did not is India's huge computer software and information technology industry.

Many Indian companies have contracts with American and European corporations to do software engineering, clerical and technical support, and other tasks over the Internet and by satellite. The Indian companies put pressure on their government to negotiate rather than fight because they were afraid that if India went to war with Pakistan, their business would be disrupted.

The story above is an example of globalization, the process by which people in different parts of the world become more and more involved with each other. How does globalization affect the way you think about your own future?

93

© 2003 J. Weston Walch, Publisher

Democracy

Democratic government not only permits, but needs, the participation of citizens in many ways at the local, state, and national level. Citizens vote, are involved with candidates for office and public issues, and discuss current events with others.

In what ways, if any, do you participate in democratic government now? How do you plan to participate in the future?

Daily Warm-Ups: Critical Thinking

94

Hotter and Dryer

Suppose the average temperature of the region where you live became 10% hotter and the average annual precipitation decreased by 10%.

What would the effect on the environment be? Which plant and animal species would grow in population? Which ones would lose population or perhaps become extinct? What would the effect on humans be?

95

Hotter and Wetter

Suppose the average temperature of the region where you live became 10% hotter and the average annual precipitation increased by 10%.

What would the effect on the environment be? Which plant and animal species would grow in population? Which ones would lose population or perhaps become extinct? What would the effect on humans be?

Daily Warm-Ups: Critical Thinking

96

Colder and Dryer

Suppose the average temperature of the region where you live became 10% colder and the average annual precipitation decreased by 10%.

What would the effect on the environment be? Which plant and animal species would grow in population? Which ones would lose population or perhaps become extinct? What would the effect on humans be?

97

© 2003 J. Weston Walch, Publisher

Social Studies

Colder and Wetter

Suppose the average temperature of the region where you live became 10% colder and the average annual precipitation increased by 10%.

What would the effect on the environment be? Which plant and animal species would grow in population? Which ones would lose population or perhaps become extinct? What would the effect on humans be?

Daily Warm-Ups: Critical Thinking

98

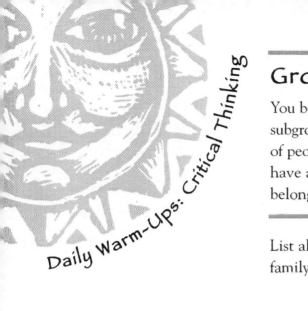

Daily Warm-Ups: Critical Thinking

Groups in Your Life

You belong to many groups. Your school is a group. Your class is a subgroup of your school. Your family is a group. A group is any set of people who interact with each other on a regular basis and who have a sense of identity—that is, the people in a group know they belong to the group. Clubs, teams, and workplaces are all groups.

List all of the groups that you and each member of your immediate family belong to.

99

Social Studies

Limits to Power

Many people in our society have power. Police officers have the power to arrest. Teachers have the power to promote students. What other powerful people come to mind?

Make a list of all the people or types of people who have power over you. Then, next to each one, list who can intervene if the power is abused. For example, you might list police officer. Next to police officer you could list police sergeant, police chief, lawyer, and judge as people who could intervene if a police officer abused his or her power over you.

Daily Warm-Ups: Critical Thinking

100

© 2003 J. Weston Walch, Publisher

Social Studies

The Money in Your Life

Think about all of the money you have received from all sources over the past year. Try to recall where it came from, where it went, and how much you still have. Approximately how much did you receive from your parents? From work? From other sources? How much did you spend on clothing, music, hobbies, gifts, eating out, or other personal purchases? How much did you contribute to family expenses? How much have you saved for future expenses, such as education, a car, or emergencies?

101

Time Line of Your Life

Draw a time line of your life. Using a ruler, draw a line about 8 inches long. Label the left endpoint 0. It represents the day you were born. Mark a point $\frac{1}{2}$ inch from the endpoint and at every $\frac{1}{2}$ inch along the line. Label these marks 1, 2, 3, and so on. They represent your birthdays. Put in a mark at the appropriate place and label it "Today." Place and label marks on the line to indicate important events in your life.

102

Map Your Life 1

Draw a map of the route that you take when you go from home to school and back. Include major streets, landmarks, and natural features on it. Plan ahead and scale your map so that it will fit on a standard sheet of paper.

103

Daily Warm-Ups: Critical Thinking

Map Your Life II

Draw a map of the route you took on the longest trip you have ever taken in your life. Plan ahead and scale your map so that it will fit on a standard sheet of paper.

104

Map Your Life III

Draw a map of the place where your oldest living relative was born. You may include an area as large as a nation or state or as small as a neighborhood, according to the information you have. Plan ahead and scale your map so that it will fit on a standard sheet of paper.

105

Map Your Life IV

Draw a map of the place where you would like to live when you become an adult. You may include an area as large as a nation or state or as small as a neighborhood. Plan ahead and scale your map so that it will fit on a standard sheet of paper.

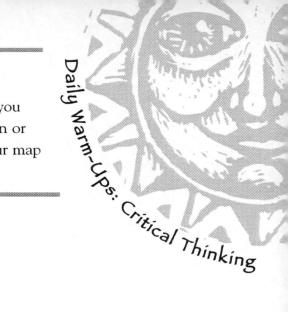

Daily Warm-Ups: Critical Thinking

106

Effects of Chemicals on Plants

Plants need water to live. What if the water has salt or acid in it?

Design and write instructions for an experiment to show how water with salt and/or acid in it will affect a plant.

107

It Glitters, But Is It Gold?

You are offered a piece of metal that looks like gold for $100. You put it on a balance and find that it weighs 32 grams, a little more than an ounce. You look up the price of gold and find that gold is selling at well over $300 per ounce. You know that real gold has a density of 19.3 grams per milliliter. Should you buy it?

Describe a procedure you could use to test whether the piece of metal you have been offered is really gold.

108

How Plants Grow

When young animals, including humans, grow, all parts of their bodies grow at roughly the same rate. Do plants grow the same way?

Design and describe an experiment to show how a plant grows.

109

© 2003 J. Weston Walch, Publisher

How to Prevent Rust

When iron or steel combines with oxygen, rust forms. There is oxygen in the air and in water. Salt water makes the oxygen combine with metals more quickly.

What is the best way to store steel wool pads to keep them from rusting? What is the best way to store steel wool pads if you want them to rust as quickly as possible?

110

Daily Warm-Ups: Critical Thinking

Science

Sorting Out Particles

Some salt, sand, and iron filings got accidentally mixed together.

Design and describe a procedure that would separate the salt, sand, and iron filings from each other.

111

When the Wind Blows

Many scientists believe that the earth's climate is changing. Climate change may affect weather patterns.

What if the average wind speed where you live tripled? Which plants and animals would do well? Which ones would do poorly? How would humans adapt?

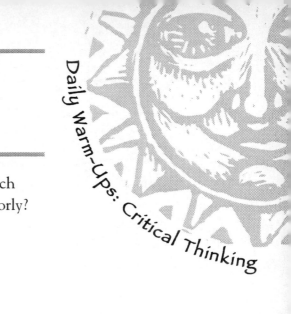

Daily Warm-Ups: Critical Thinking

112

Science

The Voyage to Mars

If the technical problems of sending humans to Mars and bringing them back safely were solved, astronauts would still face physical and psychological problems. The trip might take as long as two years. During that time, the crew would be away from their homes and families. They would live without gravity. They would live with other people in a small space with little or no privacy. And they would have nothing to look out at except the night sky.

What could be done to help solve the physical and psychological problems of astronauts going to and from Mars?

113

Growing Up Fast

When elephants are about 24 months old, they no longer need to be taken care of by their parents. They are ready to go on their own as young adults within a group. Other mammals grow up much faster: bears in about 17 months, deer in about six months, and mice in about one month.

What would our world be like if humans grew up as fast as elephants?

114

Daily Warm-Ups: Critical Thinking

Science

Learning to Survive

Animals often adapt their behavior to survive in a new environment.

Recall and write about a time in your life when you moved to a new environment—a new home, a new school, a new neighborhood—and how you adapted your behavior to live there.

115

© 2003 J. Weston Walch, Publisher

As the World Turns

Suppose the rate of revolution of the earth slowed down from one per 24 hours to one per 48 hours.

How would this change our environment and affect our lives?

116

As the World Tilts

The earth's axis of rotation is not perpendicular to the plane of its orbit around the sun. The earth is tilted about 23°.

Suppose some cosmic event caused the earth to straighten up so that its axis of rotation became perpendicular to the plane of its orbit around the sun. What would the effect be on the climate of different parts of the earth?

117

Saving Water

The water resources of planet Earth are under great pressure. There may come a point in your lifetime when water is much more expensive than it is today.

What could you and the people you live with do to use less water?

118

Science

Is the Tomato a Fruit or a Vegetable?

In 1883, the Congress of the United States levied a 10 percent tax on imported vegetables. A tomato importer named John Nix refused to pay it on the grounds that the tomato is botanically a fruit, a large berry, and not a vegetable. The case went to the U.S. Supreme Court in 1893.

If you had been one of the justices on the Supreme Court, how would you have ruled? Should Nix have had to pay the tax or not?

119

What's the Sun Doing?

R. Buckminster Fuller, a well-known twentieth century philosopher and inventor, said that we should not use the words sunrise and sunset. He said that they are leftovers from the old days when people thought the earth was flat and the sun moved around it. Today, we know that it is the rotation of the earth on its axis, not the motion of the sun that causes day and night. Therefore, he said, we should make up and use new words that express more accurately what is happening. Do you agree? If so, what words do you think we should use?

Daily Warm-Ups: Critical Thinking

120

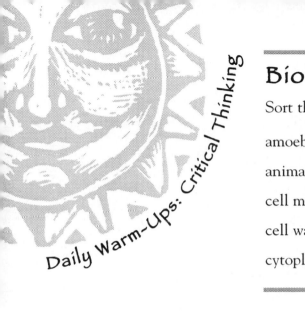

Biological Word Sort 1

Sort the words below into groups. Label each group.

amoeba	diatom	plants
animals	dinoflagellate	protists
cell membrane	fungi	stentor
cell wall	monerans	vorticella
cytoplasm	nucleus	

121

Biological Word Sort II

Sort the words below into groups. Label each group.

AIDS	mildew	spores
athlete's foot	mold	tetanus
bacteria	monerans	virus
flu	mushroom	yeast
food poisoning	penicillin	yogurt
fungus	polio	
German measles	ringworm	

122

Biological Word Sort III

Sort the words below into groups. Label each group.

ant	human	sea anemone
bird	jellyfish	spider
fish	ladybug beetle	sponge
frog	leech	tapeworm
grasshopper	mammal	tick

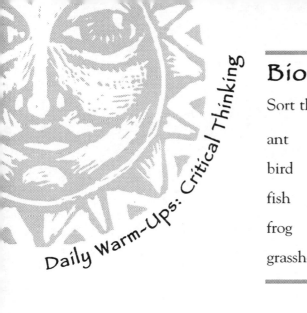

123

Physical Word Sort 1

Sort the words below into groups. Label each group.

condensation

density

evaporation

freezing point

gas

liquid

mass

melting point

solid

volume

124

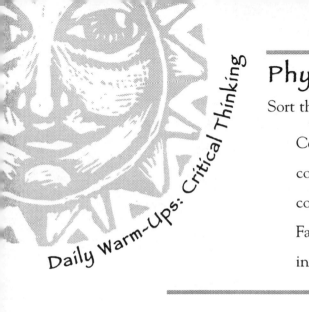

Physical Word Sort II

Sort the words below into groups. Label each group.

Celsius   matter

conduction   particles

convection   radiation

Fahrenheit   temperature

insulation   vibration

125

Physical Word Sort III

Sort the words below into groups. Label each group.

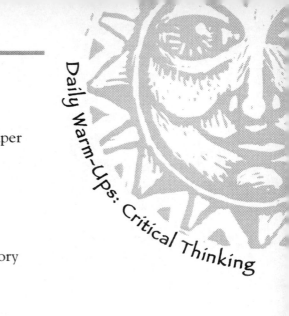

attraction	friction	sandpaper
buoyancy	gravity	ship
displacement	iron	steel
falling	magnetism	tires
field	nails	trajectory
float	nickel	
fluid	orbit	

126

Weather Word Sort

Sort the words below into groups. Label each group.

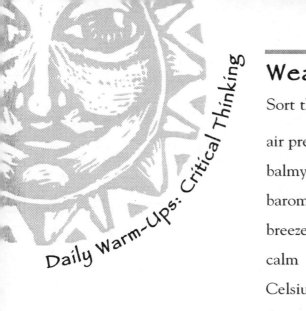

Daily Warm-Ups: Critical Thinking

air pressure	Fahrenheit	rain
balmy	freezing	sleet
barometer	gale	snow
breeze	humid	subzero
calm	hurricane	temperature
Celsius	precipitation	thermometer
degrees	psychrometer	wind

127

Energy Word Sort

Sort the words below into groups. Label each group.

atoms   fusion   renewable

cell   hydroelectric   solar

coal   natural gas   sun

collector   nonrenewable   water

dam   nuclear   wind

fission   oil   windmill

fossil fuel radioactive

Daily Warm-Ups: Critical Thinking

128

What Happened Here?

You are walking in the woods. You see the two halves of a broken, empty, light-blue robin's egg and two small feathers on the ground near a tree.

What happened here? Make a list of possible answers. Which answer do you want to be true? Which answer is most likely to be true?

Daily Warm-Ups: Critical Thinking

129

How the Heart Works

What happens when your heart beats? Below are the events that occur with each beat, but not in the correct order. Can you put them in order?

1. Blood from the body, which has little oxygen and much carbon dioxide in it, flows into the right atrium.

2. Blood from the heart flows into the left atrium.

3. Blood gets oxygen from the lungs and gives up carbon dioxide.

4. Blood gives up oxygen to cells, gets carbon dioxide, and returns to the heart.

5. The left atrium contracts, squeezing blood into the left ventricle.

6. The left ventricle contracts, pumping blood through arteries to all parts of the body except the lungs.

7. The lungs breathe out carbon dioxide and breathe in air with oxygen.

8. The right atrium contracts, squeezing blood into the right ventricle.

9. The right vetricle contracts, squeezing blood out of the heart to the lungs.

130

How the Lungs Work

What happens when you breathe? Below are the events that occur with each breath, but not in the correct order. Can you put them in order?

1. Air fills the air sacs.

2. Air goes from the throat down into the trachea and through bronchial tubes into the lungs.

3. At the ends of each of the smallest bronchial tubes, there are groups of tiny air sacs, each surrounded by capillaries.

4. Blood from the heart fills the capillaries.

5. Carbon dioxide moves from the blood in the capillaries into the air in the sacs.

6. In the lungs, the bronchial tubes divide into many smaller and smaller tubes.

7. Oxygen moves from the air in the sacs into the blood in the capillaries.

8. When you exhale air with carbon dioxide in it, it goes out the bronchial tubes, trachea, throat, nose, and mouth.

9. When you inhale, air comes into the throat through the nose and mouth.

131

Why Won't the Lamp Light?

You wake up in the middle of the night and press the switch on the lamp beside your bed. It doesn't go on.

What are the possible causes of this phenomenon? What tests would you apply to find out the cause?

Daily Warm-Ups: Critical Thinking

132

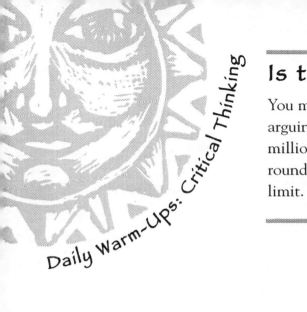

Science

Is the World Really Round?

You meet an eccentric billionaire who believes the world is flat, arguing, "After all, it looks flat, doesn't it?" He offers to give you millions of dollars if you can convince him that the world is really round. He offers you an unlimited budget for expenses and no time limit. How would you do it?

133

Outlining Species

Arrange the words below in outline form, starting with the largest group and ending with the most specific examples.

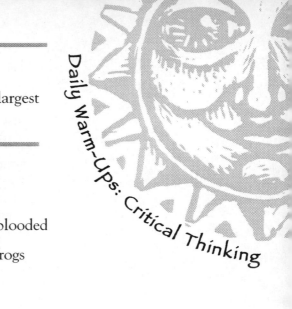

amphibians	flamingos	snakes
animals	humans	tigers
birds	mammals	warm-blooded
cold-blooded	reptiles	wood frogs
dogs	robins	
fish	salmon	

134

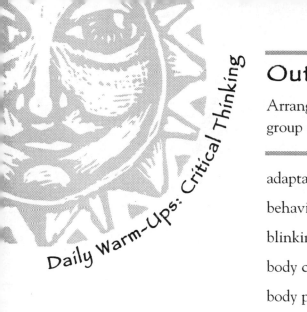

Outlining Adaptations

Arrange the words below in outline form, starting with the largest group and ending with the most specific example.

adaptations	flying	scales
behavior	fur	skin
blinking reflex	gills	teeth
body coverings	limbs	wings
body parts	migration	
feathers	quills	

135

Outlining Ecosystems

Arrange the words below in outline form, starting with the largest group and ending with the most specific examples.

air	hosts	parasites
animals	humans	predators
caribou	living	prey
dogs	mice	soil
fleas	mosquitos	water
hawks	nonliving	wolves

136

Outlining Biomes

Arrange the words below in outline form, starting with the largest group and ending with the most specific examples.

cold	hot	snowy
desert	humid	taiga
dry	many species	temperate
evergreen trees	moose	tropical forest
few trees	permafrost	tundra
grassland	rainy	windy

137

Outlining Ocean Resources

Arrange the words below in outline form, starting with the largest group and ending with the most specific examples.

cod	manganese	resources
fish	minerals	salmon
food	natural gas	salt
haddock	oil	water

138

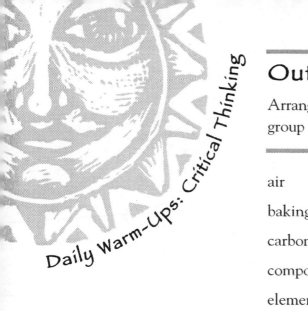

Outlining Matter

Arrange the words below in outline form, starting with the largest group and ending with the most specific examples.

air	ginger ale	sodium
baking soda	hydrogen	substances
carbon	matter	sugar
compounds	mixtures	water
elements	oxygen	

139

Forest Fire Policy

If a forest fire starts, should it be put out as quickly as possible or should it be allowed to burn? Why?

140

Daily Warm-Ups: Critical Thinking

Sun, Sea, and Plastic

Plastic is an inexpensive and versatile material that does not dissolve in water or otherwise break down or rot. It lasts for years. That's why it's used for so many things.

Plastic left on beaches, however, is a major pollution problem. Some of it is left behind by people who go to the beach; more is dumped overboard from boats, ships, and city waste disposal barges. Plastic waste—such as bags, six-pack rings, and bottles—is not only unsightly but dangerous to animals. Sea birds like gulls get caught and choked by six-pack rings. Sea turtles eat plastic bags, thinking they're jellyfish.

What can individuals, businesses, governments, and/or scientists do about plastic beach pollution?

141

Salt on the Roads

Why is salt spread on roads in winter in northern climates? What problems are associated with spreading salt on roads? What can science do to help solve the problems?

142

Daily Warm-Ups: Critical Thinking

Life Skills

Arctic Survival

You are a passenger in a small airplane that is forced to land in the Arctic.

What should you do? How long should you wait to decide? Should you stay near the plane or attempt to walk out?

143

© 2003 J. Weston Walch, Publisher

Earthquake Survival

You are in an area that has had earthquakes before. You feel the earth move under you.

What should you do if this happens when you are indoors during the day? in bed? outdoors? in a car?

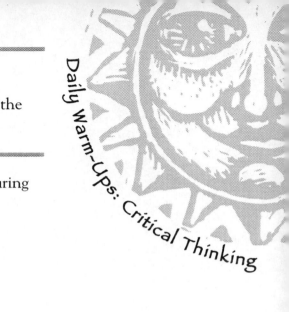

144

Life Skills

Thunderstorm Survival

You are outdoors, not near any buildings. Suddenly, a thunderstorm comes over you. What should you do to avoid being struck by lightning?

145

© 2003 J. Weston Walch, Publisher

Hurricane Survival

If a hurricane is coming, what should you do to get ready for it?
What should you do during the hurricane?

146

Life Skills

Waiting at the Mall

One of your parents has picked you up at school. As you are driving home, your parent stops at a shopping mall and tells you to stay in the car while he or she goes into the mall to buy something. Your parent does not return.

How long should you wait before doing anything? What would you do? If that doesn't work, what should you do next? If that doesn't work, what should you do after that?

147

Helping Strangers

Joel, a 12-year-old boy, says, "When you meet a stranger, you can usually tell if they're a good person or a bad one. And if you're good to people, they'll treat you well in return. So if a stranger asks me for help, I'll usually help them if I think they're okay."

Do you agree with Joel? Why or why not?

148

Home Alone

Experts on child safety say if a child comes home when no one else is there, the child should do the following:

- Check in with a parent or neighbor at once after coming home.

- Know how to call 9-1-1 in an emergency.

- Know how to use the door and window locks.

- Never let anyone into the house without a parent's permission.

- Never let a caller at the door or on the phone know that the child is alone.

- Carry a house key in a safe place (inside a shirt, pockets, or sock).

- Know how to escape in case of fire.

- Let a parent know about anything that is frightening or making the child feel uncomfortable.

149

Are you ever home alone? How often? For how long? Which of these rules do you follow or not follow?

Keeping a Friend Alive

Your best friend tells you that he or she is thinking about committing suicide.

What do you do?

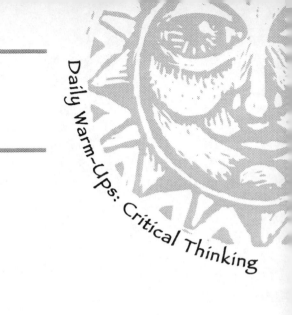

150

Sudden Travel

You have been invited to visit some friends of your family in a foreign country. You leave in one week.

What information should you find out before you go?

Daily Warm-Ups: Critical Thinking

151

Bullying

Bullying goes on in every school. Bullying includes name-calling, ridicule, false accusations meant to get a person into trouble, physical assault, theft, robbery, damage to a person's belongings, or talking about a person in a way that is harmful to his or her friendships. Bullying can sometimes be so bad that the person being bullied is afraid to go to school.

If you are being bullied, what can you do about it?

152

Life Skills

Angry Children

Good parents _____ say or do things that make their children angry.

      a. never

      b. sometimes

      c. frequently

      d. always

How would you fill in the blank? Why?

153

© 2003 J. Weston Walch, Publisher

More Angry Children

Good children _____ get angry with a parent.

    a. never

    b. sometimes

    c. frequently

    d. always

How would you fill in the blank? Why?

154

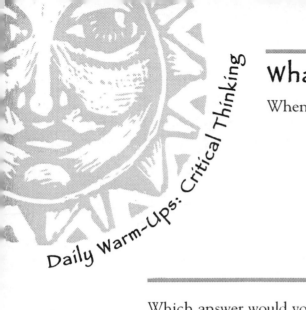

Life Skills

What to Do When Angry

When you're angry with your parents, the best thing to do is

    a. nothing. Keep it to yourself.

    b. get back at them by hurting them in some way.

    c. tell them how bad and wrong they are.

    d. tell them how angry you are.

    e. none of the above.

Which answer would you choose? Why?

155

Life Skills

Advice Column: Drinking

"I have seen my closest friend drinking beer. How can I tell if my friend has a drinking problem?"

What would your advice be?

Daily Warm-Ups: Critical Thinking

156

How to Be Popular

"The way I became more popular was by showing people the real me! That's all it took! I thought it was going to take more than that, but it didn't."

"All you really need to be 'cool' or 'popular' is friendliness or kindness. You don't have to be a supermodel that thinks she/he has to be superior among other people. That's not the way it has to be. Just be yourself, and people will admire that."

"I believe that the judgment connecting to popularity is just a human flaw. I myself am very judgmental, even though I preach against how you shouldn't do it. Come to terms that you're not perfect first, before you condemn anyone else."

157

The quotations above were posted on a web site called "How to Be Popular in High School." Which do you agree with, if any?

Choosing Friends

"Choose your friends wisely. You become what they are."

What does this saying mean? Do you agree?

158

Funny Things Happen

Funny things happen to people when they get clumped into a group. They stop thinking for themselves and surrender their wills to the group. The group takes on a mind of its own. The people in the group depend on the group to dictate what they will or will not do.

Is this true? Recall an experience you have had in which people in a group did or did not behave in this way.

159

On-line Romance

Your friend tells you that he or she is in love. When you ask with whom, your friend tells you that it is with someone he or she has never met in person but has only communicated with on the Web.

What advice would you give your friend?

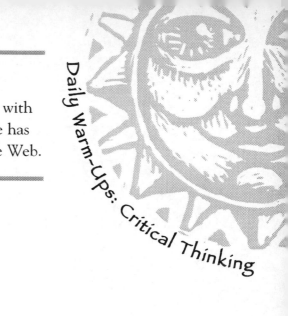

160

It's Not How It Used to Be

Your best friend, who used to be fun to be with, has changed. Now he or she is sad all the time, never wants to do anything, and has quit doing homework.

Do you continue to spend time with the friend? How do you respond to the change?

161

Inside the Teenage Brain

Jay Giedd, a neuroscientist at the National Institute of Mental Health, said the following in an interview on the PBS Frontline television program "Inside the Teenage Brain":

"Our leading hypothesis is the 'Use it or lose it' principle. Those cells and connections that are used will survive and flourish. Those cells and connections that are not used will wither and die. So if a teen is doing music or sports or academics, those are the cells and connections that will be hard-wired. If they're lying on the couch or playing video games or MTV, those are the cells and connections that are going [to] survive."

What are the implications of this for your life?

162

Daily Warm-Ups: Critical Thinking

Mnemonic Devices

Often in school, when you need to memorize things, a mnemonic device can help. A mnemonic device is something you make up to associate a word or concept with its meaning. For example, muscians use mnemonic devices to remember the names of the lines and spaces in the treble clef. From the bottom up, the spaces are F, A, C, and E; the lines are E, G, B, D, and F. The spaces spell the word "face" and the lines are an acronym for "Every good boy does fine." A mnemonic device doesn't have to make sense. Sometimes weird or foolish ones are the easiest to remember.

Make up a mnemonic device to help you remember something. If you can't think of anything, make one up for the spaces (A, C, E, F) and lines (G, B, D, F, A) of the bass clef.

163

Where You Do Homework

Here are the attributes of a good place to do homework:

- Good light

- A chair that is comfortable but supports you

- A clear working space without visual distractions (posters, knick-knacks, toys) or auditory distractions (conversations, television, radio, stereo)

- All supplies needed, such as pencils, pens, paper, ruler, calculator, dictionary

Describe the place where you do your homework. Which of the above attributes does it have or not have?

The 80/20 Rule

"The 80/20 Rule is a law of the universe. Companies do 80 percent of their business with 20 percent of their customers. Twenty percent of the workers in a company do 80 percent of the work. Individuals achieve 80 percent of their results in 20 percent of their time."

Does the 80/20 Rule apply to your life? Explain.

165

Relieving Stress

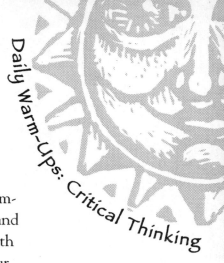

Balancing your breathing can bring immediate relief from anxiety and pressure. This technique is used in many martial arts and has been researched in applied kinesiology. Whenever you feel stressed out because of an upcoming test, game, or performance, try this. It takes about five minutes.

Go somewhere where you won't be disturbed. Sit or lie down in a comfortable place. Put your attention on each part of your body in turn and allow it to relax. Breathe through both your nose and your mouth with the tip of your tongue on the upper palate behind your front teeth.

Try this technique. Describe your experience and what results you got.

Daily Warm-Ups: Critical Thinking

What Happened Last Night?

You are walking down the hall at school on your way to class. One of your best friends rushes up to you in an agitated state and says to you with great urgency, "If anyone asks you where I was last night, say I was at your house with you. Please! Please!" and runs away.

A few minutes later, the principal stops you and says, "Come to my office right away. The police are here. They want to talk to you."

If the police ask you about your friend, what will you say?

© 2003 J. Weston Walch, Publisher

The Missing Drink

You and a friend are eating at a restaurant. The waitress brings you your sandwiches. You ask her to bring you a soft drink. Later when she brings you your check, you see that she has forgotten to add the drink.

Do you tell her? Why or why not?

168

The Missing Funds

You and your best friend are in a school club. Your friend is the treasurer. You find out that your friend has been stealing funds that belong to the club.

What, if anything, do you do? Why?

169

Making the Team

You are the captain of the soccer team and one of the better players. Younger players are trying out for the team. You know that the coach will ask for your opinion before deciding who makes the team.

Your car is not running right. You can't afford to get it fixed. One of the players trying out, who happens to be a good mechanic, offers to fix your car for free.

Do you let the player fix your car? Why or why not?

170

Life Skills

Free CDs

A friend offers you several free CDs by your favorite recording artist. You know that in the past your friend has bragged about shoplifting from record stores without getting caught.

Do you accept the CDs? Why or why not?

Life Skills

The Stolen Skateboard

Your skateboard has been stolen. You go to the police station and report the theft. The police show you a skateboard they have found that is similar to yours but not yours.

Do you take it? Why or why not?

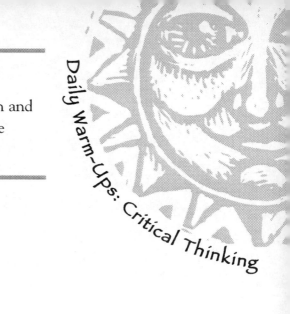

172

Daily Warm-Ups: Critical Thinking

The New Toy

You have just taken your little brother, who is five years old, on the bus to the mall and back. When you arrive home, he pulls a toy out of his pocket that he must have taken from a store.

Do you go back to the store and pay for it? Why or why not?

173

You Saw It Happen

You are standing on a corner, looking at the traffic lights, waiting to cross. A car runs the red light and smashes into another car that is crossing the intersection with the green light. As far as you know, there are no other witnesses. The drivers of the cars get out and begin arguing with each other about who is at fault. Both insist that they had the green light, but you know better. The police arrive and begin taking the drivers' information.

Do you come forward and tell the police what happened? Why or why not?

174

When You Gotta Go

At your school, there is only one girls' bathroom and one boys' bathroom. You're in class. You urgently need to go. You get permission and head down the hall. When you get to the bathroom you usually use, you are told that it is closed for repairs. The other bathroom is right next door.

Do you use it? Why or why not?

175

What Does It Mean?

Your little sister, who is in kindergarten, comes to you and says that she heard someone at school call someone else a word that is an ethnic slur. She wants to know what the word means.

What do you say?

176

Do You Tell Him?

As you enter the school building in the morning, you meet one of your teachers. His fly is open.

Do you tell him? Why or why not?

© 2003 J. Weston Walch, Publisher

Should You Peek?

You are taking an important test. You happen to be sitting behind the best student in the class. She holds her paper up so you can see it. You notice that some of her answers are different from yours.

Do you change your answers? Why or why not?

Daily Warm-Ups: Critical Thinking

178

Advice Column: So-Called Best Friend

"This is about my so-called best friend, Angela. Lately, she has been lying to me a lot. She lies about the strangest things. She told me that my friend Bob's mom is best friends with her mom. Her mom said it isn't true and that she doesn't know who Bob's mom is at all. I don't know why Angela would lie about that. That's just one of the things she lies about. She lies a lot to everyone else, too. It seems she lies to her friends more than she tells the truth to them. And the things she lies about are really lame."

What, if anything, would you advise Angela's friend to do?

179

© 2003 J. Weston Walch, Publisher

Wild Ride

You are out with a group of friends. A boy whom you don't know, but others in your group do, offers to give you all a lift in his car. You get in but soon notice that the driver is driving too fast, steering erratically, and sipping from a pint of whisky.

What, if anything, do you do?

1. The rule is: if a single vowel is stressed and followed by a single consonant (as in "bog") or a doubled consonant (as in "boggle"), then the vowel is pronounced short. If a single vowel is stressed and followed by a single consonant followed by a single vowel letter (as in "bogus"), the vowel is pronounced long. The exceptions are mostly recent imports from other languages like *fete*, which rhymes with "bet."

2. Words that end in sibilant sounds—the sounds *s*, *z*, *ch*, *sh*, and *j* that you make with your tongue up against the flat place just behind your upper teeth—add an *ez* or *iz* sound spelled *–es*. Words that end in a consonant plus *y* like country, fry, and try change the *y* to *ie*. All other words on the list and almost all nouns and verbs in English simply add an *s*.

3. Whenever the *seed* in a word is the kind that comes from a plant, it is spelled seed. There is only one word—supersede—that ends in *sede*. There are three words—exceed, proceed, and succeed—that end in *ceed*. All the others— intercede, precede, recede, secede—end in *cede*.

4. *I* before E: field, yield, shield. Except after C: receive, conceited, conceive. Or when pronounced *ay* as in "neighbor" and "weigh": weigh. Exceptions pronounced *eye*: height, sleight. Exceptions with *cien*: science, efficient, sufficient. Other exceptions: foreign, forfeit, protein.

5. Answers will vary. Here are some examples: dis-, diff-, disable, disappoint, diffuse; inter-, intersection, intermediate, intercoastal; mis-, misfire, misconduct, misuse; multi-, multiply, multilateral, multimillionaire; non-, nonsense, nonbeliever,

Daily Warm-Ups: Critical Thinking

nonstop; out- outstanding, outdistance, outscore; over-, overdo, overbearing, oversee.

6. Answers will vary. Here are some examples: -an, -ian, Iranian; -ary, -er, -ist, visionary, pitcher, geologist; -hood, -ness, boyhood, greatness; -logy, -ology, biology, astrology; -ment, advancement, pavement.

7. Here are the words we found (there may be others): careful, careless, commercial, exhaustive, exhaustion, gentleness, homeward, homeless, impressive, impression, politeness, thoughtful, thoughtless.

8. Answers will vary. Here are examples.

	-ary, -ory	-ative, -ent, -ive	-able, -ible
co-, con-	conservatory	conservative	compressible
de-	defamatory	decadent	deceivable
e-, ex-	explanatory	expedient	expendable
i-, in-	investigatory	illuminative	invincible
pro-	promontory	progressive	profitable
re-	reactionary	reflective	reproducible

9. The original sentence reads: "Livvie walked down to Lane's Cove past the post office and past Saari's, which was the only store in the village besides the market." Other good sentences are possible using the same words.

10. The original sentence reads: "A breakwater made of huge blocks of silver granite enclosed a quiet harbor for the small craft of the fishermen and lobstermen." Other good sentences are possible using the same words.

11. The original sentence reads: "He fried the fish quickly, removed the bone, put the fish between slices of bread and ate it, washing it down with milk from the carton." Other good sentences are possible using the same words.

12. The original sentences read: "She tried to go back to sleep but couldn't. Finally she got up and went to the window to look at the

twinkling, kindly stars." Other good sentences are possible using the same words.

13. We sort these words into the following sets of synonyms: acceptable, agreeable, beneficial, desirable, excellent, favorable, good; detrimental, lousy, mischievous, obnoxious, offensive, revolting; cautious, fussy, finicky; enduring, muscular, forceful, powerful, intolerable, robust.

14. We sort these words into the following sets of synonyms: art, assignment, business, calling, chore, craft, duty, employment, job, labor, occupation, profession, toil, trade, vocation; fun, recreation, sport, amusement, entertainment, delight, enjoyment, pleasure; talk, converse, speak, verbalize, chat, gab, yak; journey, proceed, move, voyage, roam, trek, explore, cruise, travel.

15. We sort these words into the following sets of synonyms: new, fresh, novel, recent; large, major, sizable, hulking, whopping, big, voluminous, great, enormous, huge, immense, vast; small, little, petite, tiny, puny, piddling, trivial; abode, dwelling, home, residence; heap, hill, mound, mountain.

16. We sort these words into the following sets of synonyms: person, individual, someone, mortal, human, soul; animal, beast, creature, fauna; distress, harass, irk, pain, stress, trouble, annoy, bother, vex; mad, rage, wrath, pique, temper, annoyance, irritation.

17. In the original story, the order of sentences was 3, 4, 2, 1. Sentence 3 is the point of the story. Sentences 4, 2, and 1 support sentence 3.

18. In the original story, the order of sentences was 2, 4, 1, 3. Sentence 2 is the point of the

story. Each of the next sentences supports the point and clarifies the sentence before it.

19. In the original story, the order of sentences was 3, 2, 1, 4. Sentence 3 is the point of the story. Sentence 2 clarifies it. Sentences 1 and 4 provide additional details.

20. In the original story, the order of sentences was: 4, 1, 5, 3, 2. Sentence 4 is the point of the story. Sentence 1 clarifies it. Sentences 5 and 3 put the point in context. Sentence 2 suggests the significance.

21. We sort these words into these six sets.
    • a, the, my, Sam's
    • really, too, very
    • beautiful, large, lovely, faint, red
    • bird, ship, handle, toothbrush, mountain, fly
    • can, will, could

    • run, see, faint, fly, procrastinate, remain

22. We sort these words into these seven sets.
    • a, this, his
    • heavy, light, green, old
    • light, water, sink, tree, bicycle, friend, fall
    • would, may, must
    • evaporate, sink, arrive, sleep, fall
    • slowly, gracefully
    • on, over

23. We sort these words into these four sets.
    • intelligent, huge, yellow, funny, empty
    • sockets, tigers, faucets, backpacks
    • walk, float, frown, collapse
    • hit, throw, dump, steal, empty

24. We sort these words into these five sets.
    • my, your, Myron's
    • incredible, black, cheap, wide, empty, crushed, admired, painted

Daily Warm-Ups: Critical Thinking

- dumpster, cannon, dress, window
- crushed, admired, painted
- and, or, but

25. Here's our paraphrase: It may be better to live a beautiful life, even if it's short, than to live a long life. There can, of course, be other equally valid paraphrases in different words.

26. Here's our paraphrase: Those who are not successful in achieving a goal are the most likely to value success the most; for example, victory in battle means the most to those who died for it. There can, of course, be other equally valid paraphrases in different words.

27. Here's our paraphrase: Jone, who wears too much makeup and has a bad reputation, acts like someone who is very pure and good. Jane, on the other hand, who is pretty and charming, turns out to have bad breath. Go figure!

There can, of course, be other equally valid paraphrases in different words.

28. Here's our paraphrase: The writer feels that looking at and admiring the stars is more satisfying than learning details about them. There can, of course, be other equally valid paraphrases in different words.

29–34. Answers will vary.

35. With the phrase "They will tell you…" the author lets you know that what the people of Coralio believe about President Miraflores is not necessarily the truth. It's reasonable to expect that the story will be about what really happened to Miraflores during the revolution and, in particular, what he did that was morally questionable and what really happened to the hundred thousand dollars. By referring to a revolution that forced the president of the

Daily Warm-Ups: Critical Thinking

country to run away in terms of "inconveniences," the author is letting you know that he will probably treat it humorously.

36. Answers will vary.

37. 0; $\frac{1}{3000}$; 4.08×10^{-4}; 0.000832; $\frac{1}{7}$; 0.3333; $9\frac{3}{4}$; 128; $76,922$; $1,000,000$; 6.28×10^{7}; 9.9838×10^{7}; 3.5×10^{9}; $8,765,243,778,625$

38. 0, $\frac{24}{407}$, $\frac{91}{635}$, $\frac{67}{302}$, $\frac{13}{41}$, $\frac{59}{180}$, $\frac{21}{62}$, $\frac{157}{400}$, $\frac{96}{209}$, $\frac{627}{797}$, $\frac{450}{463}$, 1

39. -70.060, -35.127, -26.314, -18.294, -9.686, 27.891, 46.372, 66.275, 70.757, 87.548

40. $(5 \times 900 \text{ D} + 5000 \text{ D} + 17 \times 30 \text{ D} + 432 \text{ D}) \times 1.45 \frac{S}{D}$ = Amount of shekels needed

41. The graph is very misleading. It seems to say that last year 123 students reported that they had drunk an alcoholic beverage in the preceding month and 125 said the same thing this year. However, because the total number of students increased, the percentage of students reporting drinking actually went down. Also, because a class graduated and was replaced by a new class, the group of students surveyed this year is different from last year. Furthermore, the survey is based on students' reports of drinking, not their actual behavior. Therefore, one should expect that some of them did not tell the truth in either year and that the resulting error is probably bigger than the difference between 123 and 125. The reason the increase looks big is that the y-axis of the graph does not start at zero, as it would in an honest graph; it starts at 120.

42. The proof is fallacious. The last step divides each side by $a^2 - ab$. Because $a = b$, $a^2 = ab$ and $a^2 - ab = 0$. The "proof" is an example of how dividing by 0 can lead to absurd results and is therefore forbidden.

Daily Warm-Ups: Critical Thinking

43. The probability that a coin will come up heads again after coming up heads 10 times in a row is the same as it always is when you flip an honest coin: 50%. The coin doesn't have any memory. It doesn't know what it did before your next flip. Some people reason that because 11 heads in a row is very unlikely, a coin that comes up heads 10 times in a row must come up tails the next time. This is sometimes called the Gambler's Fallacy. They forget that 10 heads and 1 tails is equally unlikely.

44. This table shows all the possible sums of two dice. There are 36. 18 of them are even. Therefore, the chances that the sum of two dice will be even are $\frac{18}{36}$ or $\frac{1}{2}$.

	1	2	3	4	5	6
1	2	3	4	5	6	7
2	3	4	5	6	7	8
3	4	5	6	7	8	9
4	5	6	7	8	9	10
5	6	7	8	9	10	11
6	7	8	9	10	11	12

The next table shows all the possible products of two dice. Again there are 36. Twenty-seven of them are even; only 9 are odd. So the chances that the product of two dice will be even are $\frac{27}{36}$ or $\frac{3}{4}$. This is because if one of the dice is even the product is even. Only if both dice are odd is the product odd.

	1	2	3	4	5	6
1	1	2	3	4	5	6
2	2	4	6	8	10	12
3	3	6	9	12	15	18
4	4	8	12	16	20	24
5	5	10	15	20	25	30
6	6	12	18	24	30	36

45. The statement is true if you assume that the order of the letters matters, that ABC and ACB are different groups. If ABC and ACB count as one group, then there are only 20 possible groups.

Daily Warm-Ups: Critical Thinking

46. There are many rectangles that fit the requirements. Here's one and its proof.

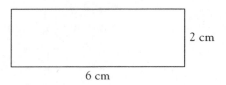

2 cm

6 cm

The area of the original rectangle is 3 cm × 4 cm = 12 cm². Its perimeter is 3 cm + 3 cm + 4 cm + 4 cm = 14 cm. The area of this rectangle is 2 cm × 6 cm = 12 cm², the same as the original. The perimeter of this rectangle is 2 cm + 2 cm + 6 cm + 6 cm = 16 cm > 14 cm.

47. There are many rectangles that fit the requirements. Here's one and its proof.

2 cm

6 cm

The area of the triangle is $\frac{1}{2}$ × 6 cm × 4 cm = 12 cm². Its perimeter is 5 cm + 5 cm + 6 cm = 16 cm. The area of this rectangle is 2 cm × 6 cm = 12 cm², the same as the triangle. The perimeter of this rectangle is 2 cm + 2 cm + 6 cm + 6 cm = 16 cm > 14 cm.

48. There are many rectangles that fit the requirements. Here's one and its proof.

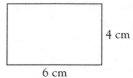

4 cm

6 cm

The area of the circle is πr^2 = π × 9 cm² ≈ 3.14 × 9 cm² = 28.26 cm². Its circumference is $2\pi r$ = 2 × π × 3 cm = π × 6 cm ≈ 3.14 × 6 cm ≈ 18.84 cm. The area of this rectangle is 4 cm × 6 cm = 24 cm² < 28.26 cm². The perimeter of this rectangle is 4 cm + 4 cm + 6 cm + 6 cm = 20 cm > 18.84 cm.

49. Answers will vary. Here's a sample.

50. Answers will vary. Here's a sample.

51. Answers will vary. Answers can be tested experimentally. An answer is correct if it works. Here's a sample.
Form a square with four toothpicks. With two more toothpicks form an equilateral triangle on the top of the square. Place the other two toothpicks so that one end of each one touches each of the two sides of the triangle that are not part of the square and forms a right angle with it.

52. Answers will vary. Many will probably include:
• Types of polygons: triangle, rectangle, pentagon, etc.
• Parts of polygons: side, vertex, diagonal, etc.
• Attributes of polygons: concave, convex, regular, irregular, similar, etc.
• Examples of polygons: wall, floor, sheet of paper, house lot, etc.

53. Answers will vary. Most will probably sort the words using the following distinctions: metric/customary, units/measuring tools, length/volume/weight/time.

Daily Warm-Ups: Critical Thinking

54. The answer to the riddle is 49. Students' riddles will vary.

55. Answers will vary.

56. Answers will vary. Here are some examples.
Prism: packages, rooms, buildings
Cube: alphabet blocks, dice
Pyramid: Egyptian pyramids
Cylinder: food cans, mailing tubes
Cone: ice-cream cone
Sphere: balls, balloons, marbles

57. Answers will vary.

58. Answers will vary.

59. Answers will vary.

60. In our numeral system, place value tells the value of each digit in a number. Each digit has ten times the value of the digit to its right. For example, 1357 means $1 \times 1000 + 3 \times 100 + 5 \times 10 + 7$. Place value extends to decimal fractions. 8.26 means $8 + \frac{2}{10} + \frac{6}{100}$.

61. Some plane figures can be arranged so that they fit together to fill up a plane with no gaps and no overlapping. That is a tessellation. For example, equilateral triangles tessellate.

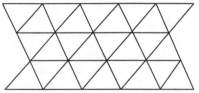

62. A rational number is a number that can be expressed as a fraction with whole numbers in the numerator and denominator. For example, $\frac{1}{2}$, $\frac{15}{13}$, $12\frac{3}{8}$. All whole numbers are rational numbers. For example, $\frac{1}{1}$, $\frac{2}{1}$, $\frac{3}{1}$, $\frac{10}{5}$.

63. To multiply fractions, first multiply their numerators. Write the product as the numerator

---

of the answer. Multiply the denominators. Write the product as the denominator of the answer. Reduce the answer to lowest terms. For example, $\frac{2}{3} \times \frac{3}{4} = \frac{6}{12} = \frac{1}{2}$.

64. To divide fractions, multiply by the reciprocal of the divisor. (Two numbers are reciprocals if their product is 1. For example, the reciprocal of 2 is $\frac{1}{2}$. The reciprocal of $\frac{5}{8}$ is $\frac{8}{5}$.) Reduce the answer to lowest terms. So to divide $\frac{6}{7}$ by $\frac{3}{5}$, multiply $\frac{6}{7}$ by $\frac{5}{3}$. $\frac{6}{7} \times \frac{5}{3} = \frac{30}{21} = \frac{10}{7}$.

65. To add fractions with like denominators, add the numerators. Write the sum as the numerator of the answer. The denominator of the answer is the same as the denominator of the fractions to be added. Reduce the answer to lowest terms. For example, $\frac{2}{7} + \frac{5}{7} = \frac{7}{7} = 1$.

66. To add fractions with unlike denominators, first write them as equivalent fractions with like denominators. To do this, find a number that is a common multiple of the denominators. (It's easier if it's the least common multiple.) For example, to add $\frac{3}{8} + \frac{5}{7}$, find a number that is a multiple of 8 and a multiple of 7. 56 is such a number. Write the fractions to be added as equivalent fractions with that number as the denominator. For example, write $\frac{3}{8}$ as $\frac{21}{56}$. ($\frac{3}{8} = \frac{21}{56}$ because $\frac{3}{8} \times \frac{7}{7} = \frac{21}{56}$ and $\frac{7}{7} = 1$. Multiplying any number by 1 gives you the same number.) Write $\frac{5}{7}$ as $\frac{40}{56}$ ($\frac{5}{7} \times \frac{8}{8} = \frac{40}{56}$ and $\frac{8}{8}$ = 1.) Add the equivalent fractions. $\frac{21}{56} + \frac{40}{56} = \frac{61}{56}$.

67. Answers will vary. Here's a sample: Fred's garden measures 14-by-19 feet. He built a 15-by-20-foot fence around it. What is the area of the ground between the garden and the fence?

Daily Warm-Ups: Critical Thinking

68. Answers will vary. Here's a sample. Leanne bought 4 T-shirts for $9.95 each. She had to pay $1.99 sales tax. After that she had $8.21 left. How much money did Leanne have to start with?

69. Answers will vary. Here's a sample. Dan gave Mario some game cards. Mario gave Dechen half of the cards he received from Dan. Dechen kept 8 of those cards and gave the remaining 10 to Rosa. How many cards did Dan give Mario?

70. Answers will vary. Using advanced mathematics, it can be proved that following these drawing rules, every map can be made with only two colors. Students cannot be expected to know this. This warm-up gives them an opportunity to think about the problem, experiment with it, and record their thoughts.

71. Answers will vary. Using advanced mathematics, it can be proved that following these drawing rules, every map can be made with only two colors. Students cannot be expected to know this. This warm-up gives them an opportunity to think about the problem and experiment with it.

72. Answers will vary. Using advanced mathematics, it has been proved that following these rules, every possible map can be made with only four colors. Students cannot be expected to know this. This warm-up gives them an opportunity to think about the problem and experiment with it.

73. Answers will vary.

74. Answers will vary.

75. About Gandhi: Mohandas Gandhi (1869–1948) was born in India and trained as

Daily Warm-Ups: Critical Thinking

a lawyer in England. He was sent to South Africa by his law firm. There, because he was Indian, he was treated as a member of an inferior race. He was appalled at the widespread denial of civil liberties and political rights to Indian immigrants to South Africa. He threw himself into the struggle for elementary rights for Indians. Gandhi remained in South Africa for 20 years, suffering imprisonment many times. In 1896, after being attacked and beaten by white South Africans, Gandhi began to teach a policy of passive resistance to, and noncooperation with, the South African authorities. Later at home, Gandhi became a leader in India's nonviolent struggle for independence from the British Empire. He lived a spiritual and ascetic life of prayer, fasting, and meditation.

See www.kamat.com/mmgandhi/

76. Answers will vary, but will probably mention sharp inequalities between men and women and parents and children.
See www.fordham.edu/halsall/ancient/asbook.html

77. The text is from "Report of an Investigation of the Peasant Movement in Hunan" written in 1927 by Mao Zedong. See www.marxists.org/reference/archive/mao/ Mao Zedong (1893–1976) was born in the village of Shao Shan, Hunan province, in China. The son of a peasant farmer, he joined the Chinese Communist Party and rose rapidly through its ranks. During World War II, he and the other Communists fought alongside the Kuomintang government, which represented the warlords and landowners who had ruled China for centuries. After the defeat of the Japanese, Mao and the Communists fought and won a civil war against the Kuomintang

Daily Warm-Ups: Critical Thinking

government. Mao ruled China as chairman of the Communist Party for decades until his death. In spite of the many cruelties and hardships the Chinese people suffered under Mao's leadership, many Chinese today think of him as the greatest figure in Chinese history.

78. Answers will vary. See www.census.gov/hhes/poverty/poverty00/pov00.html

79. This order or the reverse is the most fuel-efficient: Washington, Iceland, Finland, Syria, Pakistan, China, Malaysia, Australia, Chile, Trinidad, Tobago, Washington.

80. Answers will vary. Here are some possible headlines:
Violent Crime Levels Declining
Violent Crime Victimization Rates for Men and Women Closer Now
Source: www.ojp.usdoj.gov/bjs/glance/vsx2.htm

81. Buddhism: four noble truths, nirvana, right livelihood, Dalai Llama
Christianity: Jesus, Trinity, resurrection, New Testament, Old Testament, sacraments
Judaism: Talmud, Old Testament, Torah, Sabbath, Yom Kippur, Passover
Islam: Muhammad, Qur'an, Allah, Ramadan, hajj, Mecca
Hinduism: Veda, Krishna, Brahma, Vishnu, Shiva

82. Buddhism: Sri Lanka, China, Korea, Japan, Tibet
Christianity: Europe
Judaism: Israel
Islam: Indonesia, Malaysia, Pakistan, Iran, Iraq, Jordan, Turkey, Egypt, Algeria, Africa, Albania
Hinduism: India

83. prehistory: stone tools, hunting, fire, nomadic
Mesopotamia: Sumer, Tigris, Euphrates, Babylon, Assyria, writing, Hammurabi
Phoenicia: sea trade, alphabet
Israel: Canaan, Moses, Jerusalem, Abraham
Egypt: Nile, pharaoh, pyramid, mummy

84. India: Himalayas, Indus, Ganges, Sanskrit, Hindu, Buddhism, Chandragupta
China: Confucius, Great Wall, Han Dynasty, Silk Road, acupuncture, paper

85. Greece: Homer, Trojan War, democracy, Socrates, Athens, philosophy, Olympic Games, Sparta, Euclid
Rome: Italy, Julius Caesar, Coliseum, Latin, Christianity

86. location: latitude, 1500 Pleasant St.
place: hill, valley, lake, plain, mountain, ocean

human/environment interaction: dam, mining, farming
movement: train, road, airport
region: country, state, city, town, tundra

87–106. Answers will vary.

107. Take four jars. Put a similar plant in each one and fill it with freshwater. Put a spoonful of salt in one jar. Put a spoonful of vinegar in another. Put a spoonful of salt and a spoonful of vinegar in the third. The fourth jar, which has no salt and no vinegar in it, is the control. Be sure to label the jars. Put the jars next to a window where the sun will shine on them. Check the plants every day for at least five days. Record your observations.

108. Measure the volume of the piece of metal. Do this by immersing it in water and measuring the amount of water displaced by it. 32 grams

Daily Warm-Ups: Critical Thinking

of real gold will displace $\frac{32}{19.3}$ or about 1.66 milliliters of water. If the piece of metal displaces significantly more water than that, then it is not as dense as gold and is probably not gold.

109. Take a plant that is growing in a pot. Mark its trunk with horizontal lines one centimeter apart. As it grows, measure the distances between the marks and see how they change.

110. To slow down rust, store the steel wool pads in a dry, airtight container, like a glass jar. To speed up rust, fill the jar with salt water.

111. Spread the mixture out on a flat surface and use a magnet to pick up and take out the iron filings. Then put the salt and sand mixture in a container with water and stir it up. The salt will dissolve; the sand will fall to the bottom of the container. Pour off the water, straining it through a piece of cheesecloth or some other filter to make sure that none of the sand goes out with the salty water. Let the salty water evaporate—an oven will speed up the process—leaving the salt behind.

112. Answers will vary and will depend on the ecology of where you live. In general, plants and animals that could live with high winds would prosper and those that would be damaged by high winds would lose out. Damage to plants would hurt the animals that depend on them. Plants that use wind to reproduce by spreading pollen would especially be affected. Some human dwellings would have to be rebuilt; they could be destroyed by high winds. Some trees would have to be taken down to keep them from being blown into houses.

113. Answers will vary. Some possible solutions would be two-way video to keep the crews in touch with their families and friends; exercise machines to keep the crew's bodies from deteriorating due to lack of gravity; selection of psychologically tested couples or families who already have experience living together instead of single people; provisions of work and media to avoid boredom.

114. Answers will vary.

115. Answers will vary.

116. Answers will vary. Here are some ideas. Our habits of sleeping, eating, working, and playing are all based on a 24-hour day; that would probably change. Longer days and nights would lead to greater temperature swings each day: hotter days and colder nights. This would cause changes in the ecology which would affect agriculture, snow melting, water flow, and so on.

117. The effect would be that there would no longer be any seasons. At any given latitude, the sun would rise and set every day at the same times of day and at the same points on the horizon and climb to the same height above the horizon at noon. Higher latitudes would still be colder and lower latitudes warmer, but the temperatures at any latitude would be much closer to the average for the year. Arctic and Antarctic regions would still be cold because they would still get only indirect sunlight, but they would no longer have a six-month day and a six-month night. The sun would rise just above the horizon every day.

118. Answers will vary. Here are some ideas: Often 50% or more of household water use is for irrigation of lawns, gardens, and house plants. Use a rain barrel to capture water that runs

Daily Warm-Ups: Critical Thinking

off the roof of the house into gutters. Redirect the plumbing of the house to capture water from showers, dishwashers, and clothes washers. Use that water for irrigating the lawn, garden, or house plants. Install water-saving shower heads, faucets, and toilets.

119. In *Nix v. Hedden*, 149 U.S. 304 (1893), Justice Gray wrote for the majority, "Botanically speaking, tomatoes are fruits of a vine, just as are cucumbers, squashes, beans, and peas. But in the common language of the people. . . all these are vegetables, which are grown in kitchen gardens, and which, whether eaten cooked or raw, are, like potatoes, carrots, parsnips, turnips, beets, cauliflower, cabbage, celery and lettuce, usually served at dinner in, with or after the soup, fish or meats which constitute the principal part of the repast, and

not, like fruits generally, as dessert." The court noted that different domains of activity have different classification systems. While botanists may classify the tomato as a fruit, cooks and diners classify it as a vegetable. Imported tomatoes are still taxed.

120. Answers will vary. Of the alternative words suggested to Fuller, the ones he liked the best were sunclipse and sunsight.

121. Kingdoms: animals, fungi, plants, monerans, protists
Protists: ameba, diatom, dinoflagellate, stentor, vorticella
Cell parts: cell membrane, cell wall, cytoplasm, nucleus

122. Answers will vary. Here is one possible sort:
Fungus words: fungus, mushroom, spores, mold, yeast, mildew, athlete's foot, ringworm, penicillin

Bacteria words: monerans, bacteria, yogurt, tetanus, food poisoning
Virus words: virus, flu, polio, German measles, AIDS

123. Answers will vary. Here is one possible sort:
Invertebrates with legs: grasshopper, ladybug beetle, spider, tick, ant
Invertebrates without legs: jellyfish, tapeworm, leech, sponge, sea anemone
Vertebrates: bird, mammal, fish, human, frog

124. Answers will vary. Here is one possible sort:
Properties of matter: mass, volume, density
States of matter: solid, liquid, gas
Temperatures at which matter changes: melting point, freezing point
Changes of state: evaporation, condensation

125. Answers will vary. Here is one possible sort:
What heat is: matter, particles, vibration

Measuring heat: temperature, Celsius, Fahrenheit
Movement of heat: conduction, convection, radiation, insulation

126. Answers will vary. Here is one possible sort:
Friction words: friction, tires, sandpaper, nails
Gravity words: falling, orbit, trajectory, attraction
Magnetism words: iron, nickel, steel, field, attraction
Buoyancy words: float, displacement, fluid, ship

127. Answers will vary. Here is one possible sort:
Precipitation words: psychrometer, humid, rain, snow, sleet
Temperature words: thermometer, balmy, freezing, subzero, Fahrenheit, Celsius, degrees

Daily Warm-Ups: Critical Thinking

Air pressure word: barometer

Wind words: gale, breeze, calm, hurricane

128.   Answers will vary. Here is one possible sort:

Fossil fuel words: coal, oil, natural gas, non-renewable

Nuclear words: fusion, fission, atoms, radio active, renewable

Solar words: sun, collector, cell, renewable

Hydroelectric words: water, dam, renewable

Wind words: windmill, renewable

129.   Possible answers:

1. The baby bird hatched out of the egg while in the nest and flew away. The egg shells and the feathers blew out of the nest.

2. The egg blew or fell out of the nest and broke on the ground. The baby bird got away.

3. The egg blew or fell out of the nest and broke on the ground. The baby bird was eaten by an animal.

We want 1 to be true, but 3 is, unfortunately, quite likely.

130.   The correct order is 1, 8, 9, 7, 3, 2, 5, 6, 4.

131.   The correct order is 9, 2, 6, 3, 1, 4, 7, 5, 8.

Possible Causes	Test
Power outage in neighborhood or a wider area	Do other houses nearby have power?
No power to house	Are any other appliances in the house working?
No power to part of the house	Are other appliances nearby working? Check fuse or circuit-breaker.
No power to wall socket	Plug another appliance that you know works into the wall socket.
Broken wall socket	Plug another appliance that you know works into the wall socket.
Defective bulb	Examine bulb. Replace bulb and try. Use the bulb in another lamp that you know works.
Defective lamp	Plug the lamp into another wall socket that you know works.

132.

133. Answers will vary. Some possible approaches:
• Take him to the seashore and show him a big ship sailing away from you. Point out how the hull disappears below the horizon before the top part of the ship does.
• Show him photos of the earth taken from space that show its shape.
• Show him an eclipse of the moon or a photo of one. Point out how the shadow of the earth on the moon is round.
• Take him on a plane trip around the world. Point out how by traveling in a constant direction you return to the place where you started.
• Take him to a different latitude. Point out how the same stars appear at different heights in the night sky.
• Take him up in a space shuttle and let him look out the window.

Daily Warm-Ups: Critical Thinking

134. I. animals
    A. warm-blooded
      1. birds
        a. robins
        b. flamingos
      2. mammals
        a. tigers
        b. dogs
        c. humans
    B. cold-blooded
      1. fish
        a. salmon
      2. amphibians
        a. wood frogs
      3. reptiles
        a. snakes

135. I. adaptations
    A. body parts

    B. teeth
    C. limbs
    D. wings
    E. gills
    F. body coverings
      1. skin
      2. scales
      3. feathers
      4. fur
      5. quills
    G. behavior
    H. blinking reflex
    I. flying
    J. migration

136. I. living
    A. animals
      1. predators
        a. wolves

Daily Warm-Ups: Critical Thinking

b. hawks
2. prey
   a. caribou
   b. mice
3. parasites
   a. fleas
   b. mosquitos
4. hosts
   a. dogs
   b. humans
II. nonliving
  A. soil
  B. water
  C. air
137. I. tundra
  A. cold
  B. windy
  C. few trees

D. permafrost
E. dry
II. taiga
  A. cold
  B. evergreen trees
  C. snowy
  D. moose
III. tropical forest
  A. rainy
  B. hot
  C. humid
  D. many species
IV. grassland
  A. temperate
  B. dry
V. desert
  A. dry

Daily Warm-Ups: Critical Thinking

138. I. resources
    A. food
       1. fish
       2. cod
       3. haddock
       4. salmon
    B. minerals
       1. manganese
       2. salt
    C. water
    D. oil
    E. natural gas

139. I. matter
    A. substances
       1. compounds
          a. baking soda
          b. water
          c. sugar
       2. elements
          a. carbon
          b. hydrogen
          c. oxygen
          d. sodium
       3. mixtures
          a. air
          b. ginger ale

140. Answers will vary. Some experts have come to believe that some forest fires should be allowed to burn as long as they do not threaten human habitat. They say that forest fires help keep a forest healthy by getting rid of old, dead trees and thick bushes and allowing more sunlight and water to reach the forest floor. However, if a fire is allowed to burn, there is always the danger that it will get out of control.

141. Answers will vary. Here are some suggestions. Individuals can use less plastic and be especially careful not to leave plastic on beaches. Businesses can use other materials, especially for packaging. Governments can regulate the disposal of plastics at home and in the oceans. Scientists can try to develop plastics or other packaging materials that break down over time.

142. Water turns to ice at 32° F (0° C). If salt is spread on a road in winter when it rains or snows, the salt dissolves into the water or ice and lowers its freezing/melting point to as low as 15° F (–9° C). Thus ice on the road melts or does not freeze in the first place. This makes the road less slippery and therefore safer. Traffic can move faster. However, salt is expensive to buy and apply. It causes corrosion of vehicles and bridges. It runs off into water supplies and pollutes them and has other effects on the environment. Science can research cheaper, easy-to-apply alternatives to salt that will do a better job on the roads and avoid the side effects.

143. Cold dulls the mind. Decide what to do while you can still think clearly. It is usually best to stay with the plane. You are more likely to be rescued there. You should try to walk out only if you are fairly sure you can make it. Navigation is difficult on ice and tundra with no landmarks. Walking on ice can be dangerous. See survivalx.searchking.com/arctic.htm

144. Indoors: Drop, cover, and hold on. Drop under a sturdy desk or table, hold on, and protect your eyes by pressing your face against your arm. If there's no table or desk nearby, sit on the floor against an interior wall away

Daily Warm-Ups: Critical Thinking

from windows, bookcases, or tall furniture that could fall on you. Stay indoors until the shaking stops and you're sure it's safe to go out. In bed: hold on and stay there, protecting your head with a pillow. Outdoors: find a clear spot away from buildings, trees, and power lines that could fall on you. Drop to the ground. In a car: Slow down and drive to a clear place. Stay in the car until the shaking stops. See www.lafd.org/eqtips.htm

145. • If you are in a car, stay inside it.
      • Stay low to the ground.
      • Stay off hills or other high ground.
      • Stay out of open fields.
      • Don't stand under trees or other tall objects.
      • Stay out of water.
      • Stay off of metal objects like bicycles or farm machinery.
      See www.nws.noaa.gov/om/brochures/nh-thund.htm

146. Before the hurricane:
      • Tape or board up all windows.
      • Leave low-lying coastal areas.
      • Bring people and pets inside.
      • Bring all outdoor furniture and equipment inside.
      • Stock up on canned foods, medical supplies, freshwater (fill bathtubs), and battery-powered lights and radios.
      During the hurricane:
      • Don't use the phone unless it is an emergency.
      • Don't leave home until you hear on the radio that the hurricane has passed.

147. The most likely explanation for the fact that your parent has not returned is that the business he or she had to do is taking longer than expected. He or she will probably return soon. The best thing for you to do for a long time is nothing. Stay in or near the car. If you have waited a long time—perhaps an hour or more after your parent should have returned—and you don't have a cell phone, you might consider going to a public phone and calling a family member or a friend to report what is happening. But don't leave the car without leaving a note in the car telling your parent where you have gone and why. And don't stay away from the car any longer than you have to to make the call. You don't want your parent to return to the car, find you gone, and wonder where you are. If you are unable to reach anybody you know, you may have to go into the mall and tell a store manager or mall security about your situation.

148. Joel is wrong. To be safe, children must understand that while most strangers are decent people, *all* criminals who kidnap or abuse children, from passive exhibitionists to rapists and murderers, appear at first to be nice people. They often attempt to establish rapport with children by asking for help. They may also use bribery or flattery. Children alone in public places like fast-food restaurants and malls may be polite to strangers who ask for help but should keep their distance. Adults who really need help will and should ask other adults.
Source: www.safechild.org/strangers.htm

Daily Warm-Ups: Critical Thinking

149. Answers will vary.
Source: www.mcgruff.org/alone.htm

150. According to the National Mental Health
Association, the best thing to do is to:
• Stay with the person, unless it would be
dangerous for you. People almost never
commit suicide with someone watching.
• Listen to your friend. Let him or her talk
about his or her feelings. Don't lecture,
blame, or give advice.
• Trust your instincts. If the situation seems
serious to you, it *is* serious.
• Tell someone—an adult close to the person,
a teacher, a counselor—even if it means
breaking a promise. Saving a life is more
important.
See www.nmha.org/infoctr/factsheets/82.cfm

151. The FreeTravelTips.com web site advises you to:

• Learn as much as you can about your
destination.
• Check to see what type of weather the area
has so you can plan accordingly.
• Find out if you will need a passport or visa
to enter the country.
• Find out what types of vaccinations you
will need to enter the country; there may also
be medications you'll need to take before,
during, and even after your trip.
• Check your own medical coverage to see
what type of coverage you'll have while away
from home. Think about purchasing trip
insurance.
• Research the costs of local items so you can
set your budget. Don't forget to budget for
taxes and tipping. Many governments charge
high taxes for travel-related services.

Daily Warm-Ups: Critical Thinking

- Check the financial section of your newspaper for exchange rates.
- Build some basic language skills in the local language.
- Check the dates of local major holidays, since services may be limited on those dates. See:

www.freetraveltips.com/Foreign/Foreign01.htm#01

152. If you are being bullied, understand that it's not your fault and you don't have to take it. It won't stop until you tell somebody: a friend, a teacher, your parents, or all three. Your teacher especially needs to know what is going on. Tell him or her at a time and place when no one else will overhear you—after school, perhaps. If your teacher knows what is going on, he or she may be able to catch the bullies in the act and put a stop to it.

Meanwhile, during recess and other breaks, stay in areas where there are plenty of other people. Bullies don't like to have people watching them. On the school bus, try to sit near the driver. If you walk to school, vary your route or the times when you walk. Walk with others if you can.

See www.bullying.co.uk/children/pupil_advice.htm

153. Answers will vary.

154. Answers will vary.

155. Answers will vary.

156. According to Alcoholics Anonymous, a worldwide fellowship of people who have had problems with alcohol, someone who answers yes to even one of the following questions has an alcohol problem and needs to get help.

- Do you drink because you have problems? To relax?

Daily Warm-Ups: Critical Thinking

- Do you drink when you get mad at your friends or parents?
- Do you prefer to drink alone, rather than with others?
- Are your grades starting to slip? Are you goofing off on your job?
- Did you ever try to stop drinking or drink less—and fail?
- Have you begun to drink in the morning, before school or work?
- Do you gulp your drinks?
- Do you ever have loss of memory due to your drinking?
- Do you lie about your drinking?
- Did you ever get into trouble when you were drinking?
- Do you get drunk when you drink, even when you don't mean to?

- Do you think it's cool to be able to hold your liquor?
See www.alcoholics-anonymous.org/english/E_Pamphlets/F-9_d1.html

157.   Answers will vary. Source: www.schoolelection.com/www.popularity.com/

158–161.   Answers will vary.

162.   Answers will vary. Source: www.pbs.org/wgbh/pages/frontline/shows/teenbrain/work/

163–180.   Answers will vary.

Turn downtime into learning time!

Other books in the

Daily Warm-Ups series:

- Algebra
- Analogies
- Biology
- Earth Science
- Geography
- Geometry
- Journal Writing
- Poetry

- Pre-Algebra
- Shakespeare
- Spelling & Grammar
- Test-Prep Words
- U.S. History
- Vocabulary
- Writing
- World History